THE GROWTH OF MEDIA
IN THE THIRD WORLD

African Failures, Asian Successes

THE
GROWTH OF MEDIA
IN THE
THIRD WORLD

African Failures, Asian Successes

William A. Hachten

WITH THE ASSISTANCE OF HARVA HACHTEN

IOWA STATE UNIVERSITY PRESS / AMES

For Samuel and Carl Cotter

William A. Hachten is professor emeritus of journalism and mass com-munication at the University of Wisconsin-Madison, where he taught for 30 years. He served as director of its School of Journalism from 1975 to 1980. A specialist on international communication, he has written widely on the news media of Africa.

Authorization to photocopy items for internal or personal use, or the internal or per-sonal use of specific clients, is granted by Iowa State University Press, provided that the base fee of $.10 per copy is paid directly to the Copyright Clearance Center, 27 Congress Street, Salem, MA 01970. For those organizations that have been granted a photocopy license by CCC, a separate system of payments has been arranged. The fee code for users of the Transactional Reporting Service is 0-8138-0867-7/93 $.10.

♾ Printed on acid-free paper in the United States of America

First edition, 1993

Library of Congress Cataloging-in-Publication Data

Hachten, William A.
    The growth of media in the Third World : African failures, Asian successes /
William A. Hachten, with the assistance of Harva Hachten.—1st ed.
        p.   cm.
    Includes bibliographical references and index.
    ISBN 0-8138-0867-7
    1. Press and politics—Africa—History. 2. Press and politics—Developing countries—History. 3. Press—Africa—History. 4. Press—India—History. 5. Press—Singapore—History. 6. Press—Hong Kong—History. I. Hachten, Harva. II. Title
PN5450.H26 1993
079'.172'4—dc20   91-18204

CONTENTS

PREFACE

Newspapers, like living organisms, can grow and flourish, they can languish and wither, or they can be snuffed out. This book is about the success and failure of newspapers in anglophone Africa during the past quarter century. Subsequently, the African news media are compared with those of three Asian nations with a similar heritage of British press traditions.

Mostly, we are examining the role the press and broadcasting play in public affairs, whether as independent, critical voices or as controlled, directed instruments of government.

Without a doubt, we live in exciting times. Three major trends accelerated during the 1980s and early 1990s: the disintegration of communism, the resurgence of capitalism, and the globalization of the economy. The collapse of Communist rule in Eastern Europe and the Soviet Union, the ending of the Cold War, and the worldwide rejection of socialism as a viable form of political economy, in Africa as elsewhere, all combined to make 1989–1991 the period of the most momentous political changes since 1945. Further, the ascendency of corporate capitalism in Japan, South Korea, Taiwan, Singapore, and elsewhere has had a major impact on the world's economy.

Rightly or wrongly, many millions in Eastern Europe and the Third World came to believe that their best chances for a better life lay in democratic societies with market economies. Africa, too, has felt the ripple effects and may indeed be changing for the better. All of these changes have had profound implications for international mass communications and how we think about them.

As a teacher and scholar, I have been involved with mass communication in Africa for over 25 years—since 1963. In my first swing through Africa in 1965 during the exciting early days of independence from colonial rule, I had a chance to observe the newspapers and broadcasting systems in Kenya, Tanzania, South Africa, Nigeria, Sierra Leone, the Ivory Coast, and Senegal. In 1968, I revisited most of these new nations and also went to Morocco, Ghana, Uganda, and Zambia. Out of that experience came a book, *Muffled Drums: The News Media in Africa.* Further trips followed— a Fulbright year in Ghana, extensive research in South Africa, visits to Zimbabwe, Zambia, Botswana, Lesotho, and Sudan.

I have taught and written about Africa and its mass media throughout these years and have followed African affairs closely. During this quarter century of African independence from colonial rule, I have been impressed (and at times depressed) by the widespread failure of the news media to expand and prosper as so many Africans and scholars of Africa had hoped and expected they would.

What went wrong? Why were there just a few more daily newspapers in Africa in the late 1980s than there were in 1960? And why has there been so little freedom of the press?

The first section of this book—"False Start in Africa"—is an inquiry into the failures of media growth in independent Africa and focuses on the former British territories of Kenya, Nigeria, Ghana, Zambia, Tanzania, Zimbabwe, South Africa, and Uganda. As will be seen, the difficulties faced by publications and broadcasting seem to be directly related to political difficulties—one-party and military governments, arbitrary and repressive restraints on expression, and political instability evidenced by coups d'état, civil wars, and ethnic strife.

The media of Africa have been sharply affected also by economic stagnation—ineffective and wrongheaded centralized, socialist economies, government failures to support and encourage agriculture, misguided efforts at industrialization—as well as deeply imbedded problems of poverty, illiteracy, ethnicity, and tradition, that broad catchall concept.

I believe that reasons for these media failures can be found by looking carefully at Africa's recent history, for the starting point for understanding the press in Africa is an examination of the preindependence history of mass communication on that continent. European journalists and newspaper publishers played a central role in launching the press of Africa and in giving it the form and style that it has retained to this day. The daily newspaper came from Europe first to serve the Europeans and, to this day, largely remains an exotic and fragile import not fully integrated into African society.

The indigenous African press, which grew up in the colonial era, was important in mobilizing African public opinion, in organizing African political parties, and in aiding the struggle for political independence. But after independence, most of these newspapers

quickly succumbed, in large part, because the new African governments did not want independent and critical newspapers; thus, in
effect, the young African press was strangled in its cradle.

The years since independence have not been prosperous or politically stable times for most of Africa and its nearly 500 million
people. I have found it a dispiriting task to observe and then recount
the difficulties faced by African journalists and mass communica-
tors since the ebullient and optimistic first days of independence
during the early 1960s. I can only add that my concerns and frustrations have been shared by many journalists, editors, and broadcasters I have known in Africa over the years. Journalists of Africa
deserved better.

It is well to remember that the false start we are discussing has
occurred during a comparatively brief period—roughly 30 plus
years of African independence—and we should not be too quick to
judge or to reach final conclusions. As someone has said, Africa's
turmoil and anguish are themselves indications of its deep desires
to change and improve its lot.

COMPARISONS WITH ASIA

Several years ago, I decided that this study of the press in
former British Africa could be given added meaning if I included
comparisons with other former British colonies in Asia. One obvious
choice was India, that teeming subcontinent that is similar in some
ways to Africa.

Further, I have long been intrigued with Singapore and Hong
Kong, two islands of developmental success stories in a sea of Third
World failures. Perhaps, by learning what seemed to go right in
these two city-states and in India, I could better understand what
went wrong in Africa.

So, during 1987, my wife and I visited these three nations for a
close look at their media systems; the results for me were enlighten-
ing. Historically, all three Asian colonies had experiences similar to
those of anglophone Africa: English language newspapers serving
colonial and settler interests and the rise of indigenous papers to
express nationalism and to aid efforts toward political independence. All were influenced by English laws and institutions—and the
marvelous English language.

In recent times, the media in all three Asian nations have prospered and expanded because the economies of all three have flourished.

India today, despite its complex and intractable problems, can still rightly claim to be the world's largest democracy, with a rapidly developing economy and an expanding, outspoken, and free press that is the envy of journalists throughout Asia. Why has a free press survived in India but not in Africa?

Tiny Singapore, with just 2.6 million people, has gone from poverty and political chaos to affluence and stability in one generation. In that time, Singapore acquired a media system that by any criteria must be considered developed and on a par in media facilities and audiences with those of the West. Yet this has been accomplished in the 30 years of "soft authoritarian" rule of Prime Minister Lee Kuan Yew and his People's Action Party, which controls public communication with a heavy hand. Impressive economic and media development without freedom of expression? Yes, indeed.

Hong Kong will remain a British colony until 1997, when it will revert to the People's Republic of China, and yet it offers another kind of exception to usual patterns of communication and development. The Hong Kong Chinese, many of whom arrived as impoverished immigrants, have also gone from penury to affluence in a generation, but in a society of freedom without democracy. In the laissez-faire Crown Colony, Hong Kong residents have had no vote or effective say in government affairs, but they have enjoyed unusual freedom at the personal level to make or lose money and, overall, a great deal of money has been made.

Anyone with the resources who wanted to start a newspaper or a magazine or to make a movie or a television program has been free to do so. The results have been impressive: over 35 daily newspapers and about 400 publications and competing commercial television systems for only 5.6 million people. A few media barons such as Sir Run Run Shaw have become very rich; many others have gone broke. But within this free-trading, money-driven society has grown up one of the most diverse and comprehensive media systems in any world, First or Third.

Much about Hong Kong and Singapore is different, of course, from other new nations: both are small island city-states which lack large numbers of rural poor; both are highly urbanized and dominated by capable overseas Chinese. Hence, they lack many of the barriers to development that impede other new nations. Yet I believe that a close look at the factors that have contributed to mass communication development in Asia can prove useful in understanding why the press and broadcasting have not developed in most of Africa.

Finally, a word about the method of this study and my approach to this subject. This is not a rigorous, quantitative study in which I am trying to test particular hypotheses or theories. My data and information are not adequate for such a study. Rather, what follows is more of an extended essay, based on recent history and my own observations of Africa and Asian news media. Instead of proving propositions, I am offering certain arguments as to why I believe the press has or has not developed in those regions. I expect that some will disagree with my conclusions.

Further, I do take a normative position as to what good or effective journalism is or is not. The best journalism, I strongly believe, is that practiced by free and independent journalists who are not subject to the heavy hand of centralized, authoritarian controls. Recent events since 1985, including the rejection of the Communist, or Leninist, theory of the press, make it clear that even journalists in Moscow and throughout Eastern Europe now openly emulate this approach to journalism. Independent journalism, I further believe, goes hand in hand with democratic polities, market economies, and human rights.

A further bias is that I tend to look at this topic from the viewpoint of the journalists themselves. And most journalists I have known in Africa and Asia try to emulate this kind of open and free journalism.

Even though the governments of Africa and Asia face difficult problems and challenges, my approach reflects the skepticism and suspicion of government that has long characterized much of American journalism.

Finally, it is hoped that out of this study of the developmental and political roles of the press and broadcasting will come some additional understanding of how and why the mass media do or do not grow in today's world.

I

FALSE START IN AFRICA

1

FALSE START IN AFRICA

Just over 100 years ago, in 1885, the great powers of Europe—
Britain, France, Germany, Belgium, Portugal, Italy, and Spain—met
in Berlin to carve up the continent of Africa among themselves.
They launched the modern colonial era in Africa, and without any
Africans being present, they drew boundaries that still demarcate
African nations today.

In the century that has followed, Africa has experienced 75
years of European colonial rule and, since about 1960, well over a
quarter century of political independence or self-determination.
(Some countries, notably Angola and Mozambique and others along
the West Coast, had been under European influence and control for
several centuries.)

During those hundred years, the media of mass communication, sporadically and unevenly, moved into Africa. First came
newspapers and magazines, then radio, motion pictures, and television. The ups and downs of the African news media and the ways
that journalists there have reacted to the changing political and
social conditions have been followed and noted by scholars, journalists, and others.[1]

The final, convulsive years of colonialism, with the dynamic
nationalist and independence movements; the appearance of over
45 new African nations, usually under one-party or military authoritarianism; and then the economic false starts and reversals, frequent coups d'état, and persistent political instability—all this
change and upheaval has had a direct impact on African journalism
and mass communication.

The early 1960s were a time of great expectations for the newly independent anglophone nations of Africa, all of which took their places in the United Nations, UNESCO, and other international bodies. Decolonization was almost completed, and the new Africa was poised for the takeoff to modernity. Several of the leading nations—Nigeria, Ghana, Kenya, and perhaps Tanzania—were expected to take influential positions among the leading nations of the world.

At the same time, U.S. communication scholars confidently proposed that mass media, the "magic multipliers," could markedly facilitate and ease the great ascent to modernization and economic development of emerging Africa as well as other parts of the developing world.[2]

However, the last 20 years have been disappointing and disillusioning ones for Africa and its supporters.[3] Africa's false start in press development has belied the theories of a number of academics who had posited an important role for mass communication in bringing about social change and economic development.

Ghana, which some believed would unite and lead all of Africa under its charismatic leader, Kwame Nkrumah, has retrogressed, in part due to policies initiated by Nkrumah himself. Nigeria, the energetic giant of Africa, earlier riding the 1970s crest of a wave of oil wealth, had serious pretensions of becoming a major world power, but once again fell into the hands of the soldiers. Its economy is in shambles, and two efforts at democracy have been wrecked by corruption and ineffective government.

Tanzania's bold experiment with African socialism, widely publicized and enthusiastically supported in Africa and abroad, has foundered as well, leaving that nation impoverished, stagnant, and demoralized. All across the vast continent, many other countries suffered similar problems and recently have endured living standards lower than at independence.

The new African nations (with several partial exceptions, such as the Ivory Coast, Kenya, and Cameroon) have not prospered and neither have their media systems. One significant indication was that there were fewer daily newspapers in Africa during the early 1980s than there were during the 1960s.

NUMBERS OF DAILIES: STABILITY OR STAGNATION

With current estimates ranging from 120 to 200 dailies for the entire continent, Africa's share of the world's total of over 9,240 dailies has remained small indeed (table 1.1). And just ascertaining how many dailies have been published at various times is difficult because reliable social statistics are hard to come by for Africa. (In the following totals drawn from several sources, Egypt as well as Mauritius, Malagasy Republic, and other offshore countries are excluded.)

In 1956, near the end of the colonial era, Helen Kitchen provided a careful country by country listing of newspapers, and her count turned up 100 daily papers.[4]

Ten years later, a survey by the U.S. Information Agency found a total of 150 dailies among the same countries.[5] By 1969, Hachten reported a total of 160 daily papers.[6] A few years later, in 1975-76, Frank Barton, a leading authority on the African press, wrote that there were only 116 dailies on the continent.[7]

As of 1980, the *World Press Encyclopedia* came up with a total of 124 daily newspapers.[8] In this count, just 3 countries—South Africa with 21 dailies, Nigeria with 21, and Morocco with 10—accounted for almost half of the total among the 38 nations surveyed. Most recently, UNESCO's *Statistical Yearbook 1991* reported that there were 175 dailies on the African mainland, not including Egypt. In 16 of these nations, there was only 1 daily newspaper—usually a modest government publication.

Even allowing for the vagaries of counting papers from diverse sources, the figures show an apparently brief period of growth just before and after independence and then a slow increase in the number of dailies during the past decade or so. And this occurred when population was markedly increasing all across Africa.

Table 1.1. *Daily newspapers*

Continents, major areas	Numbers		Estimated circulation (in millions)	
	1975	1988	1975	1988
World total	7,820	9,240	450	575
Africa	170	200	5	10
North America	1,940	1,750	67	69
Latin America	1,050	1,190	23	37
Asia	2,190	3,600	128	195
Europe	2,350	2,380	211	259
Oceania	120	120	6	5

Source: UNESCO, *Statistical Yearbook 1991*, Paris: UNESCO, 1991.

Among the 10 prominent anglophone countries which are the main concern of this study, numbers of dailies either have stabilized or stagnated since the African press was surveyed during the mid-1950s. In any case, the African daily press in most countries clearly has failed to expand (table 1.2).

Table 1.2. *Numbers of daily newspapers in anglophone African nations*

	1956[a]	1966[b]	1980[c]	1988[d]
Ghana	4	3	4	4
Kenya	3	6	3	5
Liberia	1	2	2	7
Nigeria	11	18	21	31
Sierra Leone	3	1	1	1
South Africa	17	23	21	22
Tanzania	2	4	3	2
Uganda	3	4	1	6
Zambia	1	1	2	2
Zimbabwe	2	4	2	3
Totals	47	66	60	83

[a]Kitchen, "The Press in Africa," pp. 27–82.
[b]U.S. Information Agency, *Communications Data Book for Africa*, Washington, D.C.: Government Printing Office, 1966.
[c]Kurian, *World Press Encyclopedia*, pp. 34–38.
[d]UNESCO, *Statistical Yearbook 1991*, Paris: UNESCO, 1991.

For radio and television, the growth in recent decades has been more impressive, even though Africa's share of the world's totals for radio and television receivers remains quite small (tables 1.3 and 1.4). Throughout Africa, the number of radio sets climbed from 3 million in 1955, to 6.5 million in 1960, to 10 million in 1965, up to 29 million in 1975, and by 1985, to about 84 million, and to 105 million in 1989.

Television, under the same authoritarian controls, did not expand nearly as much. Late to arrive on the continent, totals for television sets went from 2.7 million in 1975 to 15 million in 1986, according to the annual *Statistical Yearbook* put out by UNESCO.

Table 1.3. *Number of radio receivers* (in millions)

	1965	1970	1975	1980	1985	1989
World Total	535	776	1,042	1,303	1,667	1,932
Africa	10	9	29	50	84	105
North America	251	305	417	471	523	551
Latin America	34	45	59	90	126	149
Asia	53	83	152	254	408	555
Europe	184	233	277	349	502	546
Oceania	3	8	13	19	24	26

Source: UNESCO, *Statistical Yearbook 1991*, Paris: UNESCO, 1991.

Table 1.4. *Number of television receivers* (in millions)

	1965	1970	1975	1980	1985	1989
World Total	186.0	298.0	407.0	557.0	688.0	797.0
Africa	0.6	1.6	2.7	8.1	15.0	21.0
North America	76.0	92.0	130.0	166.0	204.0	217.0
Latin America	8.0	16.0	23.0	36.0	56.0	69.0
Asia	24.0	41.0	54.0	97.0	137.0	190.0
Europe	75.0	144.0	192.0	243.0	268.0	290.0
Oceania	2.4	3.6	5.6	6.8	8.3	10.0

Source: UNESCO, *Statistical Yearbook 1991*, Paris: UNESCO, 1991.

This worked out to only about 25 sets per 1,000 people, compared with the worldwide average of 145 sets per 1,000 people. By 1989, totals had reached 21 million sets.

WHY THE PRESS FAILED TO DEVELOP

What went wrong? Why have newspapers and other media not expanded and prospered in independent Africa?

Economic, social, and political strictures and barriers have seriously blocked the growth of vigorous, independent *African* newspapers. From Dakar to Johannesburg, from Dar es Salaam to Accra, few newspapers owned and controlled by Africans, speaking out for the interests of other Africans free of government intrusion, have appeared and persisted.

The newly independent one-party governments were hostile to newspapers or publications they could not control. Even the small African papers that led the fight against colonialism became enemies of the new class that ruled Africa.

European-owned newspapers were particularly suspect, and many were closed down or converted into government or party newspapers. *African* journalists (whether in Nigeria, Ghana, Uganda, or Zaire, etc.) were widely persecuted and harassed by the politicians who controlled the destinies of the fragile new states.

As a result, government control of the press has done a distinct disservice to African journalism (and its readers) and has usually resulted in dull, obeisant, and uninformative newspapers. Government/party newspapers in Kwame Nkrumah's Ghana, in Julius Nyerere's Tanzania, and in Kenneth Kaunda's Zambia, to cite only several examples, have uniformly been sleepwalking automatons bearing little resemblance to the lively papers that preceded them.

The one-party state, often espousing African socialism, has failed to produce informative and effective newspapers or broadcast media. The media, instead, had become propaganda mouthpieces for increasingly unpopular regimes.

Africa's arbitrary governments have denied Africa's press a vital role in public affairs. Despite the restraints under colonialism, African papers at that earlier time were free enough to advocate special interests or causes—the *East African Standard* espousing the claims of British settlers against the aroused Kikuyus; the *Star* of Johannesburg arguing for British mining interests against the Boer Republic in the Transvaal; and most importantly, Nnamdi Azikiwe's *West African Pilot* and numerous similar papers demanding independence for West Africans from British rule, and Nkrumah's seven papers supporting his Convention People's Party in the Gold Coast.

But today Africa's kept press has had little impact on public affairs, much less on economic development or political integration.

Equally important, economic and social conditions in Africa for expanding an informed and interested reading public have not been favorable. Newspaper readership has remained mostly confined to the capitals and a few larger cities where the comparatively few educated Africans reside. Due to widespread illiteracy, poverty, malnutrition, lingustic diversity, and ethnic divisions, the majority of Africans—peasants living on subsistence agriculture and many others crowded into urban slums—remain untouched by the printed word.

Today's newspapers, often in English or French, remain "European" in that they are elite publications speaking to that minority who live in cities, are educated, literate, and generally run the government or are involved in the small modern sector. This is obviously an important audience but not the broad public; hence newspapers continue, as during colonial times, as an elite, not a mass, medium.

The absence of general economic development is a prime reason, of course, for the failure of African media systems to develop as they have in newly industrializing countries (NICs) such as India, Singapore, and Hong Kong. The only exception has been South Africa, which has industrialized but whose media were crippled and fragmented by the strictures of apartheid.

Throughout Africa, the economic and social conditions necessary for media to survive as commercial enterprises have been sorely lacking. Dearth of capital and foreign investment, scarcity of entrepreneurs willing to launch publications, and lack of available and affordable printing equipment and of trained people to put out newspapers has generally been the situation outside a few urban centers such as Nairobi, Lagos, Dakar, Harare, and those of South Africa.

Except in Nigeria and South Africa, newspapers have not been widely distributed beyond the city of publication, due to transport and road difficulties. Newspaper circulation is kept down as well by the high cost of imported newsprint, which is often rationed by governments for political reasons, i.e., newspapers that annoy the government may be denied newsprint. In television, few broadcasters have developed their own programs and films as has happened in Asia. Instead, they often rely on Western imports. Newspapers in India, too, have been subjected to government controls over newsprint. But in recent years, the Indian press has been so prosperous that it can now afford adequate newsprint, whereas the lack of paper still cripples the African press.

Private media, independent of governments, have been thwarted as well by constitutional and legal difficulties. Without effective rule of law, especially legal protection for civil liberties and private property, little hope for a free and vigorous press exists.

All across the continent—from Kenya to Ghana to Zimbabwe and South Africa—there is little protection for minority or dissident viewpoints. All were expected to "get on board" and support the government in power whether elected or imposed by a military takeover. Without a legal opposition (and there usually is not one) and the right of individual citizens to criticize their governors, the press itself has little freedom to express displeasure with the regime. The recent history of Africa is replete with the names of leaders—Nkrumah, Toure, Banda, Obote, Idi Amin, Bokassa, Mobutu, Kaunda, Ian Smith, Botha, Nimiery, Moi, and others—who would brook not even the mildest criticisms and have ridden roughshod over their critics, in and out of the press.

The disastrous economic and social situation—Africa's slide into penury—of the last 10 to 15 years has poisoned the environment needed for newspapers and other media to take hold and grow. In mass communications, as in other aspects of modern life, Africa is slipping further and further behind the rest of the world.

In looking around the world, it is apparent to me that newspapers have done best in open, democratic societies with a literate citizenry with high average incomes and under free market economies. Few countries in Africa approach those conditions. Effective newspapers that serve their readers by providing accurate and meaningful news and intelligent commentary on public affairs are rare in Africa. The few that reflect these standards are found in a few "neocolonial" centers and free market areas. Private owner-ship, Western models of journalism, and foreign investment and expertise—all appear to be important factors in producing these few viable newspapers. Only minority white South Africans had devel-oped a media system comparable to that of Western nations, but it was a system largely ignoring 84 percent of the population.

In its brief history, the press of Africa has been both an instru-ment of politics (under colonialism) and a victim of political manip-ulation and repression, especially since independence. Further, it has become apparent that the best and most effective newspapers— the survivors—from both the colonial and independence periods have been the European newspapers.

CENTRAL ROLE OF NEWSPAPERS

The daily newspaper is both the standard of measurement and the focus of this study in large part because it is the crucial medium for freedom of expression. For even in this technetronic age of tele-vision, video, cablevision, computers, and communication satel-lites, the newspaper—words printed on paper and published regu-larly—is still the principal medium for conveying significant amounts of news and public information in Africa, and indeed any-where in the world. Further, the printed word has long played a more central role than electronic communication in African politics. For, throughout most of Africa and Asia, radio and television are uniformly under direct government control, whereas the newspa-pers are at least partly independent and, by and large, are much more concerned with public affairs news and are more likely to criti-cize government activities. Print journalists usually are the strong-est advocates of press freedom and in times of crisis are the ones most likely to be jailed or repressed.

Radio has been important for independent Africa because it reaches many people, especially in remote areas hitherto largely untouched by the printed word, but it remains primarily a headline or bulletin news service. Television, largely limited to urban elites and lagging far behind radio in size of audiences, has so far, with the exception of South Africa, played a minor role as a news medium, largely because it is invariably controlled by government. Despite low literacy rates, broadcasting has supplemented but not replaced the printed word in Africa. Further, modern media in general have supplemented but not replaced interpersonal and traditional means of communication in rural Africa.

As media systems evolve and become more complex, the electronic media play a more central role in news dissemination and entertainment and take up more and more of the public's leisure time. For most of Africa, that is not yet the case.

Based on my own experience and that of Western journalism in general, an effective or "good" newspaper is defined as one that provides a wide range of news and public information that is relevant to the interests and needs of its actual or potential readership. And in order to provide useful news and information, such newspapers should be relatively independent of government or official controls. This study, then, is about the fate of *independent* newspapers. As Albert Camus wrote: "A free press can of course be good or bad, but certainly without freedom, it will never be anything but bad. Freedom is nothing but a chance to be better, whereas enslavement is a certainty of the worse."[9]

The term "free press" connotes a Western ideological bias, so we will use instead the term "independent" newspapers—publications that are relatively immune from official control, coercion, or harassment. Such a definition, it can be argued, accepts a Western normative view of the press. This is true, but then most African and Asian journalists, even those on government newspapers, hold similar values about the role of the press. African journalists aspire to and value independence and autonomy. Therefore, newspapers under direct government control and/or ownership are, by definition, not considered effective newspapers. The same can be said for party-controlled newspapers in one-party states.

Most examples will be drawn from the anglophone nations of the sub-Sahara that were once under British rule—Nigeria, Kenya, Ghana, Tanzania, Zambia, Zimbabwe, South Africa, and Uganda. This common colonial experience will provide comparisons later with other Commonwealth nations—India, Singapore, and Hong Kong. Some reference will be made as well to francophone Africa, especially the Ivory Coast and Senegal.

The African part of this study is divided into the following sections:

- A historical overview of the press during colonial rule (1885 to late 1950s). The coming of the various European publishing groups and their newspapers will be discussed as well as the rise of indigenous African publications associated with the nationalist and independence movements.
- The press and politics during the 1960s, the first decade of independence. The rise of government newspapers, the decline of independent papers, and other media changes during the crucial first years of African rule will be described against the backdrop of African politics.
- The somber seventies and eighties: the compounding political and economic difficulties of African nations and their impact on public communication. The magnitude of Africa's deep crises were becoming recognized and addressed while the media themselves seemed to play a diminished role in public affairs.
- A final section will analyze and summarize the principal reasons for the "false start" of Africa's press. Underlying these views is my conviction that the role the press has played in recent African history would seem to be at some variance with what some scholars have written about the theory of communication and development.

The wide gap between the theory, and the expectations it generated, and the reality a generation later requires a skeptical reevaluation of the following:

1. The usefulness of the Developmental Concept of the Press as found in a one-party state, whether radical socialist, conservative neocolonialist, or run by a military junta. This way of organizing mass communication to serve as an appendage or tool of government by primarily requiring the press to report news and information relating to development efforts has not resulted in media of much value to Africans nor of much help in dealing with their myriad problems. (Later, I will argue that in India, an independent and commercial press has contributed directly to development by helping Indian democracy to survive and by carrying business news and advertising that service the expanding economy.)

2. The Dominant Paradigm of the American social science approach to communication and development, so influential in the 1960s, seems to have had little impact on African development, with its formidable barriers to modernization. However, the Domi-

nant Paradigm may be relevant to such media development successes as Singapore and Hong Kong.

3. Further, the views of various critical theorists also seem wide of the mark when applied to the African context. Their critiques of Western journalism and free market mass communication have slight relevance in a region where neither approach has really been tried. In Africa, where the media have not developed, the West is blamed for keeping those nations and their media systems underdeveloped. However, such critics are silent about Asian nations where media have flourished amid strong Western influences. The critical explanations often neglect to consider the local conditions that would explain such situations.

4. Similarly, the controversy over a New World Information Order, which has largely lost its momentum in Africa, as elsewhere, has, I believe, little relevance to the difficulties of developing adequate media systems in Africa. From the perspective of recent history, the success of media development in Singapore and Hong Kong appears to be directly related to the same elements of "media imperialism" that are blamed for the failures of media growth in Africa.

5. Further, the Free Press concept has never fully functioned in Africa, although many African journalists believe in the concept and pay lip service to it. What meager progress there has been in African journalism seems related to those relatively few independent newspapers and publications operating in relatively open, market-oriented societies. This has been the case for limited periods in Nigeria, Kenya, and South Africa. Further, recent signs of hope for market economies and multiparty democracies are good augurs as well for independent newspapers.

This study's critique of various academic approaches to communication and development is analyzed in chapter 9. By looking at both the developmental and political aspects of the press in Africa, it is hoped that some better understanding of why the media do or do not prosper in Africa today may result.

2

AFRICAN PRESS UNDER COLONIAL RULE, 1885–1960

Communication is not new to Africa. African peoples, despite their great linguistic and ethnic diversity, have been communicating among themselves for a long time. The mass media, however, are not indigenous to Africa. The printing presses and newspapers, and later radio receivers and transmitters, cinema projectors, and finally, television, all initially came from Europe with the Europeans and were intended primarily for Europeans.

Modern mass communication, from the printing press to the video cassette recorder, are among many products and cultural artifacts of Western civilization that have inexorably spread throughout the world in modern times. Like railroads, automobiles, trucks, telegraphs, telephones, and legal systems, words on paper and electronic impulses on tape and film have penetrated into the non-Western world with tremendous impact. Along with technology and commerce have come ideas and ideology—John Locke, Adam Smith, and Thomas Jefferson were Westerners, as were Karl Marx and V. I. Lenin.

In journalism, not only the presses, typewriters, teletype machines, and radio broadcasting equipment, but also the practices, the norms, and the ethical standards have come out of Europe and North America. For newspapers, the page format, headlines, and the concepts of a news story—a lead, objectivity, fairness, for example—are all Western in origin. The same is true of broadcasting, where patterns of programming, the idea of a program itself, and the format of the news bulletin have been borrowed from Europe and incorporated into African practices.

At first, in most places, Africans were an eavesdropping audience. In time, two distinct newspaper traditions—European journalism and African nationalist journalism—evolved. Equally important, the practices and style of modern news presentation came with the former and were emulated by the latter. Under colonial rule, both kinds of publications had a much greater impact on politics and public affairs than did the press after 1960, the watershed year usually used to mark the end of colonial rule.[1]

These papers, whether speaking out for African nationalism, as did Nnamdi Azikiwe's *West African Pilot* in Nigeria, or for the interests of British settlers, as did the *East African Standard* in Kenya, had influence and political clout, representing views of important constituent groups when petitioning for redress of grievances or attacking policies of the colonial governments. A large portion of these newspapers, then and now, were in European languages, mostly English and French, another indication of the European impact on African journalism.

The history of the African press began long before the Berlin Conference formally apportioned the continent among the European colonizers in 1885. African, as opposed to European, journalism really began in British West Africa. The first colonial papers were started there, and the first journals published by Africans for other Africans were in the British colonies of Sierra Leone, the Gold Coast (Ghana), and later Nigeria.

The colony at Freetown in Sierra Leone was founded in 1792 by freed slaves from Nova Scotia, the first permanent outside settlers in West Africa. The *Royal Gazette and Sierra Leone Advertiser* appeared in February 1801 at Fort Thornton, near Freetown, and is believed to have been the first newspaper in tropical Africa. In southern Africa, the *Cape Town Gazette and African Advertiser* made its debut on August 16, 1800, but only lasted three months. Surprisingly, this was almost 150 years after Dutch settlers landed at the Cape of Good Hope.

In 1822, the *Royal Gold Coast Gazette and Commercial Intelligencer* was launched as a handwritten gazette in Accra, continuing as a semiofficial colonial organ, the first newspaper in the Gold Coast. The gazettes, of course, were small, official colonial government publications, and one writer said that "the genesis of African journalism lay in dry official publications of the colonial governments. The press in Africa began with publications owned and/or operated by officials."[2] The Swahili word for newspaper is *gazetti,* perhaps reflecting the fact that the first newspapers East Africans came in contact with were official publications of their colonial masters.

The first known newspaper in Nigeria was *Iwe Irohin,* handwritten by missionaries in the Yoruba language in 1859. In time, Nigeria became the major center for newspaper publishing in black Africa.

Throughout British rule, Africans launched numerous small papers, most printed but some handwritten. These appeared and disappeared, first in Sierra Leone, later in the Gold Coast and Nigeria. Publisher/printers moved freely through the three colonies, many of them playing a leading role in independence movements. James Coleman wrote that "there can be little doubt that nationalist newspapers and pamphlets have been among the main influences in the awakening of racial and political consciousness."[3]

As independence neared, African politics and newspapers became closely entwined. Nnamdi Azikiwe, a major figure of West African journalism, and his NCNC party controlled 10 newspapers in Nigeria in 1959. His longtime political rival, Obafemi Awolowo, and the Action Group had 14 Nigerian newspapers. During those same preindependence years in the Gold Coast, Kwame Nkrumah and his Convention People's Party had 7 newspapers.

Following a pattern found elsewhere in the British Empire, especially India, all three of these major political figures successfully rose to political power on the back of advocacy journalism. A total of 227 newspapers appeared in British West Africa during the colonial period—52 in Sierra Leone, 70 in the Gold Coast, 100 in Nigeria, and 5 in Gambia. Leading journalists were in many cases leading nationalists and political leaders.

Another major and lasting influence on West African journalism began in the late 1940s with the arrival of the London Mirror group of newspapers headed by the redoubtable press lord, Cecil King. The *Daily Times* and *Sunday Times* of Lagos, Nigeria, the *Gold Coast Daily Graphic* and *Sunday Mirror* of Accra, and the *Sierra Leone Daily Mail* in Freetown dominated their areas in circulation and journalistic influence. Their Fleet Street style of flashy tabloid journalism is still emulated today. The papers trained a generation of journalists and introduced modern printing methods, faster presses, and photo processing. Additional British influence came from another British press tycoon, Roy Thomson, who owned the influential *Daily Express* and *Sunday Express* of Lagos.

The Lonrho conglomerate at various times owned newspapers in Tanzania, Uganda, Kenya, and Zambia. Athough most of these privately owned European enterprises were in time taken over by independent African governments, they made an indelible and lasting impact on anglophone African journalism. In a real sense, these papers invented modern African journalism. And the small African-owned papers, used to support the fledgling political parties in the preindependence years, were clearly modelled on British newspapers.

The early press of East and Central Africa was mainly a *settler* press which reflected and supported the interests of the white man in Africa and showed little sympathy for African grievances or political aspirations. The first newspaper, the *East Africa and Uganda Mail*, was published in Mombasa in 1899, but it and its successors survived only a few years. East Africa was long dominated by the *East African Standard*, based in Nairobi, and its group of newspapers was owned and staffed by, and published for, British settlers. Long the spokesman for conservative whites, it opposed African political aspirations. Others in the group were the *Uganda Argus*, started in Kampala in 1955, and the *Tanganyika Standard*, founded in Dar es Salaam in 1930.

The first African-owned newspaper in Kenya was *Mwigwithania* ("work and pray" in Kikuyu) published in 1928 by the Kikuyu Central Association. It was edited by a young man named Johnstone Kamau, later to be known as Jomo Kenyatta, independent Kenya's first president. By the time of the Mau Mau Emergency in the 1940s, there were about 40 African vernacular papers, mostly in Kikuyu; eventually, almost all were suppressed by British authorities.

By the 1950s, European domination of the economic and cultural life of the Federation of Rhodesia and Nyasaland (later to become independent Zambia, Zimbabwe, and Malawi) was reflected in its press. Most newspapers and periodicals, including those intended for Africans, were European enterprises. Argus South African Newspapers controlled the *Rhodesian Herald* and *Sunday Mail* of Salisbury, the *Chronicle* and *Sunday News* of Bulawayo, and the *Umtali Post*.

The Argus company entered Northern Rhodesia (later Zambia) in 1951 when it purchased the *Northern News* from Sir Roy Welensky and turned it into a daily, the first in the Protectorate. The paper became the *Times of Zambia* in 1965, with British journalist

Richard Hall as editor. Lonrho, a British conglomerate, later took over the *Times of Zambia* and the Sunday *Zambia Mail.*

In British-ruled Africa, it was almost axiomatic that the greater the number of settlers in a colony, the less freedom was allowed to local Africans to have their own newspapers, lest they use them for political purposes. Africans living in Northern Rhodesia had almost no involvement in journalism. This was in marked contrast with anglophone West Africa (with its British civil servants but few settlers), where numerous African journalists played an important role in public affairs and politics.

In South Africa throughout most of this century, the Argus group of newspapers and other English-speaking newspaper proprietors, notably the South African Associated Newspapers (SAAN), developed the best newspapers on the continent—based on private ownership and English newspaper traditions and know-how and financed by British mining interests. That tradition continues today, despite accelerating attrition in the apartheid conflict, through their leading publications, including the *Star* of Johannesburg, the *Sunday Times,* the *Cape Times,* the *Cape Argus,* and others. The Afrikaans-language press groups, Perskor and Nasionale Pers, long closely tied to the ruling Nationalist Party, became in recent years better news media and somewhat more independent of the Afrikaner oligarchy that still rules South Africa.[4]

The black press of South Africa has had a long history, much of it quite separate from the white or European newspapers. The separateness of the black press was a result of South Africa's racial segregation and long predated National Party dominance and apartheid legislation. White newspapers simply ignored the non-white majority. A South Africa editor commented:

> A look through the newspaper files of the prewar years and indeed, through the 40's, is a revealing exercise. A visitor from another planet, going through these pages, day after day, year after year, would get the impression that South Africa was a country populated almost exclusively by 3,000,000 whites. There is almost no reference at all to black people—except occasionally in the odd crime report, or in some general allusion to "the Native Problem."[5]

As a result, nonwhites had their own newspapers, and between 1836 and 1977, more than 800 publications were written by or aimed at Africans, Coloureds, or Indians in South Africa. Some were small, ephemeral newsletters of only two to four pages; others, with white publishers, were full newspapers or magazines with circulations up to 170,000. Nowhere else in Africa was the indigenous, nonwhite press as diverse, widespread, and sophisticated as in South Africa.[6]

In the vast, thinly populated territories of French West and Equatorial Africa, colonial policy did little to encourage indigenous African newspapers or even the conditions (adequate education and freedom of expression) that might make such papers feasible. Until the mid-1930s, newspapers and journals could only be published by French citizens. Moreover, while the circulation of publications from France was encouraged, there was a tax on the import of presses and newsprint into French Africa. This was a further deterrent to African newspaper development.

The most successful and lasting newspapers were published in Dakar, the administrative center of *Afrique Ouest Française,* where there was a concentration of European traders and colonial officials as well as educated Africans. *Le Réveil du Sénégalais* was founded in 1885, *Le Petit Séngalais* in 1886, and *L'Union Africaine* in 1896, but these were essentially newspapers published by Frenchmen for other Frenchmen.

Abidjan in the Ivory Coast was the locale for the first newspaper owned and operated by Africans themselves. *Éclaireur de la Côte d'Ivoire* appeared in 1935 and was an immediate success with African readers. The years between 1945 and 1960 saw a flurry of press activitiy in Abidjan, with some 36 papers appearing and disappearing. As in British West Africa, this was related to the highly fluid political situation whereby Africans were permitted for the first time to organize political parties and to vie for political power. After independence, all these papers went under after one-party governments took over.

Perhaps of more significance was the appearance during the 1930s of the Charles de Breteuil newspaper chain, the only group of its kind in French Africa and a powerful voice for French colonial interests. *Paris-Dakar* started as a weekly in 1933 and became a daily in 1935. In 1938 *France-Afrique* (which became *Abidjan-Matin* in 1954) appeared in the Ivory Coast. *Le Presse de Guinée* began in Conakry in 1954 and *La Presse du Cameroun* in 1955. These de Breteuil papers were originally edited for European readers, with the exception of *Bingo,* a popular picture monthly for urban African youth, started in Dakar in 1952.[7] De Breteuil's *Abidjan-Matin* was the Ivory Coast's only daily newspaper during its first four years of independence. It later became *Fraternité-Matin,* the official (and only) daily paper in the newly independent nation. This was a trend followed in other new African nations, much to the detriment of press independence and diversity of political views.

Even though these early European newspapers in Africa—whether in Dakar, Abidjan, Accra, Lagos, Nairobi, Salisbury, Dar es Salaam, Kampala, or Lusaka—were published by colonialists for European settlers and expatriates, often reflecting the most unattractive aspects of colonialism, they did bequeath to these fledgling nations a tradition of independent newspapers standing up to authority and speaking for a constituency, however narrow and self-serving.

Further, several generations of African journalists learned their trade on these papers. In British Africa, African journalists absorbed not only professional techniques of reporting and editing, but also the values of British press freedom. At the same time, these nationalists were claiming all the rights of Englishmen, including the right to speak out and print one's grievances without governmental interference and, in time, the right to self-government. African journalist/politicians effectively used the printed word to speed and ease the historic process of decolonization.

Even today, in various African capitals, the residual influences of these European papers can still be discerned.

By the end of the colonial period, the press, spurred by the lively political jousting of various political parties, showed a surprising vigor and diversity.[8] This was not to last.

Journalists and others would soon learn that political independence from the colonial rule of Whitehall or the Quai d'Orsay and the resulting majority (i.e., one-party) rule by African oligarchies was not the same thing as personal freedom. African journalists soon found that self-determination aside, they were less free than before to speak out on public issues or even to engage in the business of publishing a private newspaper or journal.

3

THE EXCITING SIXTIES

The atmosphere of Africa in the early 1960s was well described by a British correspondent, Xan Smiley:

> In the heady days just after independence, Africa beckoned. The natural wealth and beauty, then as now, were enormous. How easy to tap them. A few crash programs to combat illiteracy and disease; the transformation of the cream of the new generation into black white men at universities in the United States, Britain, and France; the education of the masses; and presto! Outsiders wanted to use African ports, build airfields and make friends.[1]

On the eve of independence, the foreign-owned newspapers of colonial Africa were generally considered residual European appendages that had done little to serve the needs or interests of the great African majorities. Surely, it was felt, with Africans running their own affairs and with majority rule based on popular support, the Africans' own newspapers and other media would expand and thrive along with the young nations themselves. The new governments promised extensive literacy programs and expanded education. The excitement of independence politics, it was believed, had fostered widespread interest in news and public affairs among urban Africans.

These expectations, however, have not been borne out; the press has not prospered, just as the new nations themselves have not prospered.

The decade of 1960–70 was a crucial period for the press of

Africa. As self-rule came to colony after colony, the need for more public communication and newspapers appeared obvious. Instead, newspapers remained small and undercapitalized, circulations were limited and advertising revenues sparse, trained journalists were hard to come by, and potential readership was sharply constrained by illiteracy and poverty.

By the late 1960s, Daniel Nelson, editor of the *People* of Uganda, wrote, "What is noteworthy is not that a few papers have been born or that circulations have been going up but that so few newspapers have been born and that sales have increased so little."[2]

Important changes, however, did take place in the patterns of ownership and control of newspapers. To a large degree, the new African governments themselves assumed ownership of both newspapers and electronic media, establishing a pattern that has characterized African media to this day.

Increasing government involvement was evident in several trends of the 1960s: a decline in the number of independent newspapers, both African- and European-owned; the appearance of numerous government newspapers; expansion of government ministries of information; nationalization of radio and television broadcasting services; and the widespread establishment of government news agencies that would control news flow in and out of the new nations.

In country after country, the pattern was repeated. Private or independent newspapers, often lively and partisan and which had nurtured the independence movements, were increasingly harassed by the new governments, which showed little tolerance for free expression or contrary views. In Zambia, Sierra Leone, Ghana, Nigeria, and elsewhere editors were often fired from their jobs, jailed, or forced into exile.

It was Ghana, the former Gold Coast, which became the acknowledged trendsetter for black Africa and set the pattern of mass communication for much of independent Africa. Its first president, Kwame Nkrumah, pledged a major role for mass communication and was the first African leader to bring the media under his personal control.

Nkrumah started the first national news agency in black Africa, the Ghana News Agency; launched the first government newspapers; and eliminated his press opposition by buying out the British-owned *Daily and Sunday Graphic* and shutting down his most outspoken critic, the independent *Ashanti Pioneer*, and jailing its editor, Kwame Kesse-Adu. He expanded the British-initiated government information services, developed radio broadcasting, and finally, launched a television service—just before he was deposed by a military coup in February 1966.

Nkrumah espoused a revolutionary role for the press in his quest to lead the continent toward a united and socialist Africa. He wrote, "Just as in the capitalist countries the press represents and carries out the purposes of capitalism, so in revolutionary Africa, our revolutionary press must represent and carry forward our revolutionary purposes."[3] Nkrumah's ideology was to influence other African leaders and provide a rationale for one-party control of public communication. To many African journalists, however, such talk was the death knell of what little press freedom Africans had earlier enjoyed. Journalists and broadcasters in Ghana, and elsewhere, became subservient civil servants, doing the bidding of politicians.

For the media of Ghana (and later, much of Africa), the significant factor was not the socialist ideology so much as the direct government involvement in public communication. This paralleled state intrusion in the economy, to the detriment of national development. (As we will see later in India, the press there also has been subjected to government interventions, but these harassments have been much more sporadic, and the Indian press has still managed to maintained its legal freedoms. And in Singapore, Lee Kuan Yew interfered with the press much as Nkrumah did. But in Singapore, media prospered because the economic policies were sound, whereas Nkrumah's policies decimated Ghana's economy.)

The chief characteristics of Nkrumah's widely emulated authoritarian pattern of mass communication were (1) near complete government control of all instruments of public communication; (2) media constantly exhorting the public to support government policies and actions; (3) the press given little independence or access to government news; and (4) the press forbidden to directly criticize the leadership or to publish dissenting views.[4]

With such a paradigm, the reasons for the decline of the numbers of newspapers were obvious. The one-party or military governments demanded conformity and were intolerant of dissent and criticism. New African leaders were particularly suspicious of the remaining European-owned papers. Furthermore, most new nations lacked both entrepreneurs and capital to launch new papers, particularly in such uncertain political conditions.

Scarcely any new independent papers appeared, and there was a steady attrition of those that remained. Two of the London Mirror group's papers, the *Daily Mail* of Freetown and the *Daily Graphic* of

Accra, each the dominant paper in its country, were sold to the new governments of Sierra Leone and Ghana, respectively.

A few years later, the third Mirror paper, the successful *Daily Times* of Lagos, ended up in the control of the government of Nigeria. After the Nigerian military coup of 1966, Lord Thomson of Fleet closed down his lively *Daily Express* and *Sunday Express* of Lagos, which were gaining circulation while losing money.[5]

In those optimistic first years of independence, the proliferation of government or party newspapers was the most significant trend in African journalism. (In one-party states, a party newspaper was often indistinguishable from a government paper.)

In Nigeria, the federal government established its own group, the *Morning Post* and *Sunday Post* in Lagos, and each of the three regional governments did likewise: *Daily Sketch* and *Sunday Sketch* in the Yoruba-dominated Western Region, the *New Nigerian* in the Hausa/Fulani Northern Region, and the *Nigerian Outlook*, in the Ibo-controlled Eastern Region, which briefly became the *Biafra Sun* during the Nigerian Civil War.

During independent Nigeria's first exuberant years (1960 to 1966), the young nation enjoyed an unusual period of press diversity, if not freedom, because neither the federal government nor any of the three regions could dominate the rest of the country. The resulting public discourse was enlivened by the clash of ideas coming out of press voices of the different political entities. However, it can be argued that the often irresponsible, contentious papers exacerbated the rising level of political violence that ended with the first military coup in January 1966.[6]

Elsewhere on the continent, Julius Nyerere's ruling TANU party in Tanzania, concerned that it lacked a direct voice in the press, launched a weekly paper, *Uhuru*, on Independence Day, December 9, 1961. (In 1965, *Uhuru* became a daily.) TANU's English language daily, the *Nationalist*, followed in 1964.[7] In addition, the *Tanganyika Standard*, the old settler-owned paper, was nationalized as the *Standard* and was made an official government mouthpiece. Later it became the *Daily News*. As a result of these shifts, no independent voices remained in the press; all spoke for the party and government.

In neighboring Zambia, the government took over the *Central African Mail* and turned it into the *Zambia Mail*. The other daily, *Times of Zambia*, formerly owned by Lonrho, also became state controlled.

Francophone Africa never had much of an independent press, and even that shrank during this period. The experience of Guinea was typical: the all-embracing grip of Sekou Toure's PDG party resulted in bringing virtually every medium of communication under its direct supervision.

By the end of the 1960s, the influential de Breteuil newspaper group had pretty much dropped out of sight. *Dakar-Matin*, founded by de Breteuil in 1933, ceased publication in 1970, replaced by a new national daily, *Le Soleil du Sénégal*, with the government as principal shareholder. In Abidjan, as mentioned, the Ivoirien government's attractive new offset daily, *Fraternité Matin*, replaced de Breteuil's ailing *Abidjan-Matin*.

As the decade ended, Sudan's President Gaafar al-Nimeiry announced the nationalization of all newspapers and local news agencies in Sudan, an authoritarian pattern that continued for 16 years.

By 1970, the new look of African journalism had become clear: government- or party-controlled newspapers had taken center stage; white- or European-owned papers gradually withered away except in Kenya, Rhodesia, and South Africa; the few independent African-owned papers, such as the *West African Pilot* and the *Nigerian Tribune* in Nigeria and the *Pioneer* of Ghana (revived after Nkrumah's fall), were barely hanging on while many small, irregular publications disappeared along with political oppositions.

The exception in black-ruled Africa was Kenya: two foreign-owned newspapers, *Daily Nation* and *East African Standard*, continued to flourish under the one-party government of Jomo Kenyatta.

Everywhere political intrusion into newspaper operations made it increasingly difficult for journalists to do their jobs. As a result, a large proportion of African newsmen simply left journalism or, often, their country. By the late 1960s, London harbored quite a number of former African newsmen forced to quit and go abroad. Editors were particularly vulnerable to political pressures. For example, after each successive coup in Ghana, the top editors of the papers were fired as the papers suddenly switched their support to the latest group of unelected rulers.[8]

Africa's hopes for a vigorous, independent press really disappeared along with legitimate political oppositions. The right of the press to criticize public affairs is directly linked to opposition political parties or interests. If a legitimate "loyal opposition" exists in or out of a government or legislature, then the press usually enjoys the privilege of reporting what that opposition has to say. But under one-party or military rule, opposition voices were not tolerated in or out of the press.

Journalist David Lamb summarized what had happened to the press of Africa:

> In almost every country of Africa, the prime role of the media is to serve the government, not to inform the people. This press is a propaganda vehicle, used to manipulate and organize and control; any questioning voice is a potential threat and only the government is wise enough to know what the people need to know. Here is how an official communique from the Republic of Somalia defines the role of the press: "It is the function of the nation's mass communication media to weld the entire community into a single entity, a people of the same mind and possessed of the same determination to safeguard the national interests."[9]

Thus, well before other problems began to surface, the free or independent press was perhaps the first of Western-style institutions to fall. Lamb said the controlled press was the tool the governments most needed to manipulate the minds of the uneducated masses. "News was censored and managed to the point that what got into print was little more than government news releases," Lamb wrote.[10]

The frustrations of African journalists were well expressed by a leading Kenyan editor, Hilary Ng'weno: "In respect to the all pervading power of government, nothing has really changed from the bad old days of colonialism. Only the actors have changed; the play remains the same. Instead of a colonial governor, you have a President or a field marshal. . . . Newspapers were taken over and those which were totally opposed to being incorporated into the government propaganda machinery were closed down."[11]

Government ownership and/or control of most instruments of mass communication thus became the norm in independent Africa, an inevitable outcome of one-party governance or of military regimes, which often took over after a coup. In sum, most postcolonial countries had acquired or established during the 1960s the major newspapers, all radio and television broadcasting, a national news agency, and an extensive government information service—all under official control and directly accountable to those in power. That accountability required unquestioning support of the nation's leaders and their policies and persistent exhortations to the public to do likewise. In the circumstances, most newspapers and broadcasters practiced self-censorship, avoiding criticism of government and leaving any dissent or growing discontent among the people without even meager outlets.

Unlike with the once entrepreneuring newspapers, independence did not bring any real change in the control of broadcasting. From its beginnings, radio, a major source of information and news, has been controlled by central authorities, whether colonial or post-colonial. The history of African radio and television services has in general been one of subservience to the interests of the ruling elites.[12]

The prevailing pattern of mass communication followed closely the Developmental Concept of the Press.[13] The evolving rationale or justification for this press concept emphasized that:

1. All instruments of mass communication must be mobilized to deal with the great tasks of modernization—illiteracy, poverty, hunger, political integration, and overall economic growth. Government must step in and provide a media service when no other institutions exist to do so, as was the case in most of Africa. This concept reflected the hopes and high expectations of economic development, urged on by international agencies, such as UNESCO, and financed by foreign aid from Western nations.

2. The media should support authority, not challenge the government in place. Little or no leeway is permitted for dissent or criticism of the national effort.

3. Information, in effect, becomes the property of the state, and as a scarce resource, information must not be squandered in frivolous fashion but must be conserved to further the national interest. This approach implied a paternalistic attitude toward the right to communicate—the government will decide who will use the facilities of mass communication and, on occasion, will determine what will be said.

This model of mass communication, clearly authoritarian, was close to that of Communist press theory, with its emphasis on mass media as a tool or instrument of official policy.

Indeed, echoes of Lenin's views on the press were heard in Nkrumah's exhortations to the "true African journalist":

> His newspaper is a collective organizer, a collective instrument and a collective educator—a weapon first and foremost to

overthrow colonialism and imperialism and to assist total African independence and unity. . . . The true African journalist
very often works for the organ of the political party to which he
himself belongs and in whose purpose he believes. He works to
serve a society moving in the direction of his own aspirations.[14]

Graham Mytton commented that it was easy to understand why
so many journalists and broadcasters ran into difficulty with Nkrumah's government. It was not for them but for the ruling CPP to
decide what best promoted the goals Nkrumah outlined.[15]

This basic African developmental pattern, honed in Nkrumah's
Ghana, was emulated throughout Africa, with and without Nkrumah's neo-Communist ideology.

Dennis Wilcox observed that this theme of developmental journalism took several variations:

One African notes, "The role of the press is to mobilize the
masses around precise objectives." An Ethiopian diplomat says,
"The Press should improve the quality of education in a country." The press in Sierra Leone is charged with "unifying the
country." The role of the press in Togo is supposed to "inform
and form" and "mobilize the people behind the president and
the party." The same is true in Zaire where "the role of the journalist is to help educate the masses and rally support for the
government." The Sudan is pursuing national development
along socialist lines and "the press is used by government to
promote and disseminate the socialist way of nation building."[16]

Despite the variations of emphasis and ideology, it all added up
to authoritarian control of public communication.

As we have seen, the newly imposed political barriers to independent journalism arrived with the new African governments. But
certainly, media expansion and growth were also stymied by the
lack of an economic base in most countries to support publications
and broadcasting as well as the absence of a large, literate, and
comparatively affluent public to participate in an expanding system
of mass communications.

4

THE SOMBER SEVENTIES AND EIGHTIES

During its first 25 years of independence, Africa was caught up in a deepening crisis of profound political, economic, ecological, and social consequences. Predictions made in the late 1980s about Africa's future were increasingly gloomy. No solution to the myriad problems seemed apparent or available.

Olusegun Obasanjo, former president of Nigeria, said it clearly in 1988: "The bold fact is that Africa is a continent in dereliction and decay. We are moving backward as the rest of the world is forging ahead."[1]

The noted French agronomist Rene Dumont had earlier warned: "Most of the countries of tropical Africa, with one or two exceptions, are up to their ears in debt, without any hope of ever being able to repay what they owe. Twenty years after independence these countries are in reality bankrupt, reduced to a state of permanent beggary."[2]

Concluding his survey of post-independent Africa, Martin Meredith commented:

> The World Bank noted in a 1983 report that despite billions of dollars of international aid poured into Africa, the region faced a "deepening crisis." A 1983 study of the Economic Commission for Africa, attempting to look 25 years ahead, made particularly chilling reading. It predicted that, based on existing trends, poverty in rural areas would reach "unimaginable dimensions," while the towns would suffer increasingly from crime and desti-

tution. "The picture that emerges," it said, "is almost a night-
mare."[3]

Yet, there was nothing sudden or abrupt about this slide; the
signs had long been there but became particularly apparent during
the 1980s.

Political disarray was an early symptom of crisis and was characterized by numerous coups and abrupt changes of governments
with military regimes often replacing civilian governments. The initial efforts at Westminster-type parliaments and multiparty rule
were generally abandoned. Old-fashioned authoritarianism took
over in nation after nation.

During the "first dance of freedom," of about 25 years, more
than 70 leaders in 29 nations were deposed by assassinations,
coups, and purges. Among 41 major independent nations, only 7
allowed opposition political parties. Seventeen were one-party
states and another 17 military regimes.[4] The 44 new nations were
rocked by 20 major wars and 40 successful coups between 1957
and 1981.

Civilian or military regimes were all too often tarnished by corruption, incompetence, and just bad policies. One-party governments or military juntas were often unresponsive to public opinion
or to the needs and desires of their peoples. This was true under
even the most reputable leaders, such as Julius Nyerere of Tanzania. "Self-determination" became a kind of bad joke, since the average African had little input into his own government's policies and
usually had no way to vote a government out of office.

Consequently, a coup d'état was the usual path to change. Free
and open elections were scattered and rare. "One man, one vote—
one time" became a sardonic expression frequently repeated.

Many nations were in effect ruled by oligarchies based on ethnicity. In Kenya, the Kikuyus had replaced the British and enjoyed
all the "perks" of civil service jobs, university positions, land ownership, etc. In a similar fashion, the Shonas under Robert Mugabe
dominated an independent Zimbabwe. In Zimbabwe's media,
ZANU or Shona views predominated, and the minority Ndebeles
were effectively denied access to the media. In early 1988, Mugabe's
ruling ZANU party merged with Joshua Nkomo's ZAPU party with
the hope of ending the ethnic strife in which an estimated 3,000
Ndebeles had been slain by government forces. Thus Zimbabwe too
was moving from a parliamentary democracy to one-party rule.

Tribal animosities were largely responsible for genocidal civil wars in Burundi, Uganda, Central African Empire, Equatorial Guinea, and elsewhere. Nigeria's civil war of 1967–68 had its roots in ethnic rivalries between the Ibos and Hausas.

Persecution of minorities, based on long-standing ethnic rivalries, was a creeping disease. Arabs were driven out of Zanzibar, Indian merchants and technicians out of Uganda, and whites from Angola and Mozambique. In South Africa, the persecuted, some 26 million Africans, were actually a majority of the population.

George Ayittey, an expatriate Ghanaian, wrote:

> As a black African, I am ashamed to see how our own leaders in Africa indirectly aid and abet apartheid. Take one look at how black African leaders treat their own black African people. More than 600,000 Lango and Acholi tribesmen perished at the hands of Amin, Milton Obote, and Tito Okello in Uganda. In 1972, the Burundi government, run by the Watusi minority (15% of the population) decided to massacre every educated Hutu (the majority). Within two months, more than 200,000 Hutus were slain, their homes and their schools destroyed. In all these barbaric atrocities, the Organization of African Unity (OAU) did nothing, shamefully nothing.[5]

In 1988, genocide flared up again in Burundi, where the government reported that at least 5,000 were killed in the uprising of Hutu peasants against the ruling Watusi minority.[6] News service reporters put the death toll several times higher.

Despite years of apparent self-determination, these tribally based oligarchies were usually arbitrary and unconstitutional governments. Civil rights and property rights enjoyed little protection of law, subjected instead to the whims of political expediency. African governments in general showed little tolerance or concern for minorities, especially if those minorities represented different ethnic or tribal groups.

When the Commonwealth Heads of Government met in October 1987 for its biennial attack on South Africa's apartheid system, Amnesty International issued a report citing human rights abuses among African nations. Kenya was charged with "a deliberate program to silence or intimidate its political opponents, including torture of detainees" by keeping them in waterlogged, underground cells until their skin rotted. Nigeria was accused of public executions in which victims were killed "by successive volleys of bullets fired at intervals, starting with shots aimed at the ankles" and proceeding upward. Zambia and Zimbabwe were singled out for ille-

gally detaining large numbers of political opponents and then tor-
turing the prisoners.[7]

Political instability had economic roots, of course, and the accompanying economic crisis was exacerbated by the steady decline
in food production, due in large part to the general neglect of agriculture. Economically, the new Africa generally failed to grow, and
according to the UN Council on Africa, the economies of 30 of 49
independent African countries have gone backward since 1974.

The average African in 1991 was poorer than he was in 1970.
According to World Bank data, average per capita GDP (gross domestic product) has declined by about 4.5 percent since 1970.

Africa has been called the continent most in need of intensive
care. Roughly 280 million of its estimated 650 million people are
regarded as poor by anybody's standards. The poorest of the poor
live mostly in sub-Saharan Africa: black Africa minus South Africa
and Namibia. Richard J. Barnet wrote that

> with the fastest growing population in the world and with a
> gross national product only about the size of Belgium's, sub-
> Saharan Africa is caught up in a process of development charac-
> terized by environmental destruction, political corruption, and
> dimming prospects for the poor majority. A senior AID official
> pronounced all of sub-Saharan African, with a few enclaves ex-
> cluded, to be a "basket case" and told me that pouring substan-
> tially more foreign money into the region would do no good
> whatever. Corruption, mismanagement, and the persistence of
> tribal politics all conspire to direct well-meant subsides into the
> wrong pockets, much of the money ending up in numbered ac-
> counts in Zurich banks.[8]

Nor was there much social justice. Advocates of decolonization
assumed that the end of empire would bring about increased equality. But this did not happen. According to the International Monetary Fund, something like 1 percent of Nigeria's population in 1980
controlled 75 percent of the nation's oil wealth. Corruption, graft,
and waste were rampant in many of the new nations where a new
class of party functionaries, politicians, and well-connected entrepreneurs built fortunes.[9]

Some of the new rulers flaunted their wealth. When oil began
gushing in Gabon, the president built himself a $650 million marble
palace with revolving rooms and walls that disappeared at the
touch of a button. The emperor of the Central African Empire, one
of the world's poorest nations, collected nine palaces at home—one

for each wife—and a mansion in France, and spent $10 million on his own coronation. Corruption-ridden, decaying Zaire had a debt of over $5 billion, but its president, Mobutu Sese Seko, was reported to have a personal fortune of about $6 billion.

A U.S. diplomat identified the major reasons for the economic crisis as:

1. Inappropriate domestic economic policies based on an over-reliance on the public sector and inadequate attention to private sector development and free market factors. ("African Socialism"—with its bureaucratic centralization, social engineering, and parastatal corporations—could point to no successes anywhere in Africa.)

2. Disastrous neglect of the all-important agricultural sector, in which over 75 percent of all Africans are employed. In order to stay in power, African governments kept food prices low to keep urban people happy, and thus farmers had little incentive to produce. (Although mostly agrarian, Africa was losing the ability to feed itself. In 1984, 140 million of its 531 million people were fed entirely with grain from abroad. In 1985, that number may have reached 170 million. The United Nations reported that 10 million people had left their villages in search of food. Starvation deaths had exceeded 1 million.)[10]

3. Population explosion. Africa has the highest population growth rate in the world—over 3 percent. Population increases have tended to wipe out any modest gains in living standards and have directly contributed to the ecological crises and famines of recent years.

4. Rapid buildup since the 1970s of African external debt with the accompanying heavy economic burden of debt servicing. From 1973 to 1983, Africa's medium- and long-term debt rose from $14 billion to $66 billion.[11] By 1988, Africa owed almost $218 billion, nearly half its domestic product and twice its export earnings, according to the UN Economic Commission for Africa.

Rampant population growth has outstripped not only living standards but also literacy, so that the actual percentage of illiterates has increased as well as the total number of illiterates. Schools, health services, water, electricity, and other urban support systems deteriorated badly as many of Africa's capitals—Lagos, Kinshasa, Khartoum, and numerous others—swelled with urban slums.

Further, almost without exception African governments have allowed a crucial part of their colonial inheritance—the infrastructure of roads, railways, cities, and towns built by Europeans—to deteriorate badly. Roads built by European engineers have been gradually swallowed up by the bush. At independence in 1960, Zaire had 58,000 miles of good roads; by 1980 only 6,200 miles were passable.

Health care to deal with a wide variety of tropical diseases has long been a challenge for Africa. The latest threat comes from AIDS. By the early 1990s, the AIDS epidemic was spreading rapidly in Africa despite prevention campaigns started by every nation. The deadly virus has hit particularly hard the young adults in the cities. For example, in Kampala, Uganda, and in Lusaka, Zambia, more than 20 percent of the adults are infected. Ominously, AIDS has spread rapidly from cities to rural areas where most people live. In contrast to the United States, AIDS in Africa is spreading mainly through heterosexual intercourse, striking men and women alike, the rich and the poor. Social effects of the plague are predicted to be more devastating in Africa than anywhere else in the world.

The problems of population growth and agricultural decline were complicated as well by the ecological crisis generated by soil erosion, deforestation, and excessive cropping. The widespread drought and famine of 1973–74 in the Sahel region, then the devastating drought and famine of 1983–85 that affected Ethiopia, Sudan, and much of central Africa, and similar conditions in 1988 were tragic evidence of these ecological realities.

By 1992, the harsh truth was that in much of Africa, the people were poorer than in 1960. They suffered from drought, disease, dependency, demographics, and debt.[12]

As Mort Rosenblum wrote, "No one can measure the blood spilled. But *South* magazine, in August 1986, cited nearly four million dead in sub-Saharan Africa since 1960 from wars, massacres and famine resulting from armed conflict."[13]

IMPLICATIONS FOR THE MEDIA

During this slide into penury, which became so clear after 1980, the role of Africa's mass media was thoroughly circumscribed. Because of near complete government control of public information, the kept press of independent Africa could only function as a cheerleader supporting unpopular leaders and their policies, no matter how wrongheaded they might be.

Despite extensive foreign aid and numerous development plans and schemes, as well as centralized official control of mass communication, the media certainly did not play much of a role in national development. The press and broadcasting were not utilized effectively to aid development projects: they were used principally to help maintain increasingly unpopular elites in power. This experience seemed to refute the purported role of the developmental concept of the press.

The few remaining independent African papers, so important in forming public opinion in the late colonial period, were largely muted. And they were few indeed. By 1978, only five countries in sub-Saharan Africa had any newspapers that were not owned or controlled by the government—Gambia, Kenya, Liberia, Rhodesia, and South Africa—and all of these were under varying pressures of self-censorship. And in recent years, press freedom has diminished in each of these countries as well.

The last foreign-owned papers, such as both the *Daily Nation* and the *Standard* in Nairobi, had to walk a fine line drawn by self-censorship in order to survive. This was also true for the Argus-owned papers in Zimbabwe before they were nationalized in 1982.

During these troubled times, the press was either unable or unwilling to report what was happening, thus failing to provide a forum for exchange of ideas and opinions between the rulers and the ruled.

Such restraints on news about Africa's disastrous famines has probably cost lives. The drought and famine in Ethiopia, which made world headlines in 1985 and again in 1988, brought in a good deal of Western relief aid, but it had been unreported in that country for at least two years. One observer noted: "Actual starvation began to ravage the country as early as 1983. Relief agencies knew it. Many Ethiopian officials knew it, but the government banned any reporting of the oncoming catastrophe in its own media until late 1984. Even when the ban was lifted, coverage had to focus on government 'relief and rehabilitation' efforts, not on the famine itself." [14]

In neighboring Sudan, Mike Kilongson, a Sudanese journalist, was forced to flee to Kenya in 1986 after he had been imprisoned and tortured by the authorities following his reports for the BBC about the famine in the Sudan. On the other hand, there has rarely been a famine in a country with a free and active press. This is not to say that there is any causal relationship between press structure and the conditions that produce famine. But in nations with independent newspapers, famine conditions are more likely to be reported, and hence, the government (and the international aid community) are more likely to act to avert starvations.

(It has been suggested that India's free press is a major factor in heading off famines in that country. For, as soon as there are any starvation deaths, however small the number, the Indian press can spread the news and create pressures on the government to act on the problem.)

But under Africa's controlled media, little feedback went up to the increasingly autocratic rulers. The African press failed to inform the public about the deepening crisis. The government-controlled papers, despite their socialist rhetoric, did not serve the new societies well.

Xan Smiley pointed out how the stifling of dissent in black Africa militated against effective government: "The leader, all too often sheltered within a circle of sycophants, loses touch with his people."[15] In 1982, Smiley wrote, "There is virtually no domestic press in Africa worthy of the name." With several partial exceptions (South Africa, Nigeria, and Kenya), he added, "Elsewhere on the continent, politicians can expect their activities to be glorified rather than interpreted by native journalists, and most begin to believe the publicity, though most of them are also sensible enough to have numbered bank accounts in Zurich, just in case the unthinkable should happen."[16]

Heavy self-censorship became a standard feature of Western reporting about Africa as well. A sense of guilt and the hope of returning to report again cause many reporters to pull their punches and not report to the full extent how badly things have gone in Africa. "Above all," Smiley wrote, "if he is to survive in respectable journalistic circles, he must paint over rank incompetence, cruelty, and corruption of the new elites—be they right wing or left wing—and ignore the amorality and inertia among the common people."[17]

Those African journalists and publications which were courageous enough to speak out often became the targets of repressive actions. Idi Amin shut down the Ugandan press, harassed and killed several journalists, and banned all foreign reporters. In 1986, one of Nigeria's leading journalists, Dele Giwa, editor of *Newswatch,* was assassinated by a car bomb—a few days after being interrogated by the state security service.

Critical journalists have had a hard time in Ghana, and their papers are often closed down. "It is very unfortunate," said Elizabeth Ohene, the first woman editor of a Ghanaian newspaper, "that so many governments in Africa believe that journalists should be part of the political process. . . . This is dangerous both for government and the press, because the people need to know that, in the last resort, they can turn to the press to defend them against official abuses.''[18]

Nonetheless, in some African nations, despite periodic clampdowns, independent newspapers do manage to persist. Nigeria's tradition of lively and outspoken papers has endured, despite the country's adversities and periodic military rule. Some consider that Senegal, which has 62 newspapers and publications (but only one daily paper) ranging from right wing to Marxist, to have the most lively press in sub-Saharan Africa.

Broadcasting's role was also muted—everywhere thoroughly under the control of the urban-oriented oligarchies controlling the regimes. Radio has long been a mouthpiece for government. Local radio reached many more Africans than the press, but its contribution to public affairs and news was minimal. Most radio news was a bulletin board of official handouts, usually leading off with an item of praise for the head of state. This has been called protocol news.

A few exceptions to this pattern can be found. Africa No. 1, a French language station based in Libreville, Gabon, is in broadcasting to make money and has attracted a continental audience of 15 million with a lively, fast-paced format. Moreover, it has the rare reputation for news accuracy, with news and commentary clearly separated.

Television, much less developed than radio, has had even less impact and has not lived up to its potential. With a few exceptions, it has become a government mouthpiece and a showcase of American reruns. Nigeria recently celebrated its 25th anniversary of broadcasting, and according to one observer, there was evidence that television has enlarged, rather than diminished, the gap between rich and poor, urban and rural.

> And instead of nurturing traditional cultural values, television has eroded them by offering a large amount of imported programming. Those who need information on development most, the urban poor and rural population, are usually not reached by television. . . . Television takes the lion's share of limited communication budgets, so there is little money left to be spent on other media that are more effective in reaching those with the greatest need for information and development.[19]

Further, political restraints have hindered television's development. "Few governments have encouraged the kind of freedom of expression in the media that would enable the urban poor and rural populations to better understand and articulate their needs."[20]

In the face of such debilitating social, economic, and political conditions, the growth of mass media and an increase in readers and listeners seemed largely out of the question.

Increasing illiteracy, inadequacies of education, widespread poverty, endemic disease (complicated by the devastating new plague of AIDS), and malnutrition—all of this means that except for a few urban elites, the potential readers and listeners for the media were just not there. If a new paper is launched, the problem is how to distribute it outside the city of publication when mail service is so erratic and the road and rail systems so chaotic and unusable.

Private capital to launch new journals and papers is largely nonexistent. Most of the best independent newspapers throughout the world have flourished in free and open societies where private property was protected by law and where newspapers were profit-making ventures in market economies. In those mostly Western (or Westernized) societies, investment capital was available to the publishing entrepreneur willing to take the risk of putting out a newspaper.

But in most African societies, with a few exceptions, such economic conditions and entreprenuers were notably lacking. Even when capital was available, few entrepreneurs were prepared to take the political risks of starting newspapers.

The economic and social conditions prevailing, for example, in such capitals as Bamako in Mali, Addis Ababa in Ethiopia, Conakry in Guinea, Niamey in Niger, Freetown in Sierra Leone, and Kampala in Uganda, during the past 25 years have not been hospitable to fledgling newspapers of any sort. Neither African one-party nor military rule permitted free and unfettered political discourse, nor did the economies offer much promise of return on investment.

For example, in March 1987, a bold experiment to publish an independent newspaper in Tanzania collapsed just hours after the first issue of the paper, *Africa Baraza,* rolled off the presses. Copies of the new weekly—the *first* to be launched in postindependent Tanzania by a private businessman—were seized and confiscated by police. The paper was reported to have been selling "like hotcakes" before the police arrived.

But the picture of journalism and mass communication in contemporary Africa is not completely bleak. In several nations on the continent, the press is well established, although still harassed.

5

OUTLOOK

Despite the hostile environment for independent journalism throughout much of Africa, several partially successful media stories stand out. Kenya, Nigeria, and South Africa, each in its own way, have been battered by afflictions shared by most African states, but nevertheless, their media have shown vigor and resilience. Each of them have urban centers—Nairobi, Lagos, and Johannesburg—with the critical mass of literate urban elites and economic activity needed for media enterprises to flourish. But how long either the economic or political base for vigorous journalism can remain stable under current conditions is in question for each nation.

KENYA

Under the firm yet astute leadership of Jomo Kenyatta, Kenya's "founding father" and first president, Kenya did not cut its ties with Britain and encouraged a free market economy. Consequently, Kenya prospered while its neighbors, Tanzania and Uganda, sharply declined. As a one-party government, Kenya has had a national news agency, Kenya News Agency, and a government-controlled radio and television service, the Voice of Kenya.

But Kenyan journalism has been unique in black Africa because both its two major daily newspapers, the *Standard* (the last survivor of the East African Standard Group, now owned by the

Lonrho conglomerate) and the *Daily Nation* (launched by the Aga Kahn) were foreign owned and between them provided some of the best journalism north of the Limpopo River. The *Nation* group also publishes *Taifa Leo*, a Swahili version of the *Daily Nation*, as well as the *Sunday Nation*. (By 1990, both groups were partly owned by Nairobi businessmen.) The *Standard* group also puts out the *Sunday Standard* and a Swahili weekly, *Baraza*. These are not government or party newspapers, and they do a creditable job of reporting African as well as world news.

What they do not do well is report on the domestic politics of Kenya; they are susceptible to political pressures and exercise much self-censorship. The papers do not report in depth or criticize President Daniel arap Moi, just as they did not attack Kenyatta or any members of his family. In 1982, the editor of the *Standard*, George Githii, was fired because of an editorial that criticized the government for detaining people without trial. The editor of the *Daily Nation* suffered a similar fate on another issue.

Despite their journalistic quality, the *Standard* and *Daily Nation* are not indigenous African newspapers, and that is something Kenya sorely needs. Yet Nairobi has been the venue for the most successful group of private publications launched on the continent by an African without either government or foreign capital assistance. This has been due to the efforts of Hilary Ng'weno, who grew up in the slums of Nairobi, studied physics at Harvard, became a reporter and then editor of the *Daily Nation*. From there he went on to establish the only African-owned and -managed independent newspapers and magazines south of the Sahara. His publishing house, Stellascope Ltd.—which began with a humor weekly, *Joe*, in 1970—has published *Weekly Review, Nairobi Times, Rainbow*, and other magazines, and proved that indigenous journalists could compete with both government and foreign publishers.

However, his *Nairobi Times*, an afternoon paper aimed at the educated elites, was bought out by the Moi government and turned into a KANU party morning newspaper, the *Kenya Times*. So for the first time, Kenya had a government newspaper, and this was later joined by the *Sunday Times* and a Swahili daily, *Kenya Leo*. President Moi established a publishing partnership with the late British publisher Robert Maxwell, and the *Kenya Times* was upgraded to a full-color tabloid, its circulation jumping from 30,000 to 70,000, passing the *Standard's* 49,000.

Kenya, which earlier had been a hopeful focal point of democracy and capitalism in Africa, has recently become overwhelmed by a failing economy and a burgeoning population. The population has been growing at a disastrous 4 percent a year, the highest in the world. Its 1984 population of about 20 million will have doubled in 17 years and then double again after 17 more years, reaching an expected 83 million people by 2025. This ominous trend places tremendous pressures on limited land, housing, food, and jobs, leading to rising political discontent. Per capita food production is down 38 percent in Kenya since 1952. The political pressures on President Moi have been tremendous, and he has responded with severe repression and curtailment of free expression.

Numerous journalists and editors have been jailed or detained for either political or journalistic activities. Kenya's leading writer, Ngugi wa Thiong'o, spent most of a year in prison for a novel published in English which depicted Kenya's elites as exploiters of the common people. In 1982, more than 3,000 people, including the entire 2,100-member air force, were arrested after an attempted coup. Kenya's democracy is clearly on the decline as Moi has assumed more dictatorial powers, including the right to appoint and remove judges.

The outlook for Kenya's relatively free press and its fragile democracy is not promising. The *Weekly Review*, noted for its trenchant commentary on politics, has quieted down after the government urged advertisers to boycott Ng'weno's paper. And in 1989, the *Daily Nation*, still the best-selling paper with 165,000 circulation, was banned indefinitely by Parliament from reporting its proceedings. The paper was accused of misreporting Parliament, promoting dissident views, and being disrespectful of Kenya's leadership.

Some journals of political opinion have often had great influence in African nations and thus come into conflict with repressive governments. One recent example is *The Nairobi Law Monthly*, which was launched in 1987 by editor-in-chief Gitobu Imanyara and has since grown to over 15,000 circulation. After three other similar journals were banned in 1988 and 1989, the *Law Monthly* remained one of the few critics of the Kenya's drift to dictatorship and called for democratic reforms. The Moi government reacted sharply, banning the paper frequently and twice arresting Imanyara. After again calling for a return to multi-party democracy, he was arrested a third time in 1991. Finally in December 1991, bending to international and domestic pressures, President Moi reluctantly agreed to scrap one-party rule and to hold elections. And so in January 1992, more than 100,000 people attended Kenya's first legal anti-government rally in 32 years and heard speakers call for an end to the "bad dream" of one-party rule.

Kenya, however, was still a long way from having real democracy and freedom of expression.

NIGERIA

Nigeria has been called the "giant of Africa" for more than its 356,669 square mile size. A dynamic and heterogeneous population, the largest in Africa, plus abundant resources (especially oil), gave it real promise of modernization and economic viability. Further, it has had the most extensive media system in black Africa, with long traditions both of press freedom and indigenous African journalism. Because of its size and diversity, Nigeria has had the "critical mix" needed to make a media system work.

Many observers felt that "as Nigeria goes, so goes Africa." And as with most of Africa, Nigeria has not been been doing very well. After 30 years of independence—marked by six military coups and two turbulent periods of mismanaged civilian rule—Nigeria currently faces deep economic problems and more military rule but hopes to try democracy once again by 1993. (However, Nigeria's hopes for a speedy return to civilian rule were undoubtedly set back by an attempted coup on April 22, 1990, which failed after 11 hours of fighting between military forces in Lagos.) During a long binge of corruption and misrule, fueled by its oil wealth, Nigeria neglected its agriculture, imported its food, saw its living standard plummet, and went deeply in debt as an estimated $5 billion was looted from the public coffers by corrupt government officials. The lively press pointed out these problems but to no avail. Twenty years ago, Nigeria had serious pretensions of becoming a major world power; today, Nigeria is just struggling to again become a viable nation.

As with Kenya, Nigeria's hopes for recovery are complicated by a soaring population. At independence in 1960, there were 52 million Nigerians; by 1984, there were 94 million; and by 2025, the population is projected to be 329 million!

Despite the buffeting it has taken from a succession of repressive soldier/rulers, the Nigerian news media have survived in large part because a great many Nigerians do believe in independent newspapers that will report the news and criticize their governors. The British value of press freedom grew deeper roots there than anywhere else in Africa. Even though the Nigerian newspapers look like Fleet Street tabloids and affect English titles, such as "Times," "Guardian," "Vanguard," "Punch," "Tribune," "Express," Nigerian journalism is lively, irreverent, assertive, and very much West African in tone. Before independence, Africans published over 100 newspapers in Nigeria, and this probably explains why the Nigerian press is so Africanized today.

Except for South Africa, no nation approaches Nigeria in the number and variety of its newspapers. In 1986, there were 19 dailies, of which 8 were privately published. In addition, there were 37 Sunday and weekly papers, bringing a total of 56 papers published in such scattered cities as Lagos, Kaduna, Ibadan, Kano, Jos, Owerri, Aba, Onitsha, Calabar, Benin, and Zaria.

Daily circulations of the leading dailies in 1986 were *National Concord,* 180,000; *Daily Times,* 160,000; the *Guardian,* 150,000; *Vanguard,* 160,000; and the *Punch,* 110,000. Sunday papers had even higher sales: *Lagos Weekend,* 300,000; *Sunday Concord,* 220,000; *Sunday Guardian,* 190,000; and *Sunday Times,* 180,000.[1] Although 24 of the 56 publications were federal or state controlled, there was still a refreshing variety of viewpoints coming from varied and scattered sources. Without doubt, the Nigerian press has more diversity than any in Africa. But even its adherents would agree that the Nigerian press stresses opinion and advocacy much more than information, and to get a somewhat rounded view, a reader must peruse a variety of papers, as many urban Nigerians do.

Radio and television broadcasting also varies from the African norm of one centralized government broadcasting system. Nigeria, a pioneer in both radio and television, still leads the way. Reflecting political and ethnic balancing, broadcasting is a joint responsibility of state and federal governments, with a strong emphasis on regional autonomy, unusual in Africa. Nigeria's federal political structure fosters 32 television stations, 11 under different state governments, and 21 under national control. Each of the 19 states has its own radio station, and the Federal Radio Corporation of Nigeria (FRCN) serves the nation as a whole with a variety of services. Radio, decentralized as it is, broadcasts in a wide range of vernacular languages.

Still, Nigerian journalists have had to deal with a variety of repressions and harassments in recent years. In 1983, for instance, the *Sunday Concord* published official reports that the police considered embarrassing. Its editor, Dele Giwa, was detained under the official secrets act and spent several spells in prison. Ray Ekpu, a *Concord* columnist, was arrested and charged with murder after he satirized the practice among some public officials of burning down public buildings to cover evidence of embezzlement and fraud. The day after his column appeared, the tallest building in Lagos, head-quarters of the External Communications Authority, caught fire, killing several people. In his column, Ekpu suggested the blaze was inevitable and he was arrested. After 16 days in prison, he was cleared of all charges. The *Guardian,* another independent paper, termed the treatment of the two journalists "police harassment" and an "abuse of public office" that "opens the way to tyranny."[2]

Under the subsequent harsh, 20-month rule of General Muham-madu Buhari, the press suffered further setbacks. Decree Number 4, proclaimed by the Buhari regime in March 1984, set heavy penal-ties for publication of unauthorized information about public offi-cials. In June 1984, two journalists with the *Guardian* were jailed for a year for publishing a story predicting changes in Nigeria's for-eign service. Just before the bloodless coup in August 1985 that replaced Buhari with General Ibrahim Babangida, at least 12 jour-nalists were in jail and authorities had threatened to close inde-pendent papers "that got out of hand."[3]

The most notorious incident, and one embarrassing to the latest military ruler, General Babangida, occurred in October 1986. Dele Giwa, who left the *Concord* to become editor of the newsmagazine *Newswatch,* was killed by a powerful package bomb sent to his home. Some suspected Nigeria's military intelligence, which had interrogated him. Others pointed to corrupt businessmen and drug dealers. The killing remained unsolved and became a cause célèbre with the Nigerian public, eliciting thousands of letters to *Newswatch.* On November 8, 1986, the day of Giwa's funeral, all Nigerian newspapers came out with black-bordered mastheads.[4]

The press's continuing outspoken response to this and other clashes with authority, whether civilian or military, only underlines the continued vigor and courage of a press that values its freedom and refuses to give in to official repression.

Nigeria's press will be given more breathing space if democracy does indeed return as the military rulers have promised. On July 4, 1992, Nigerians went to the polls for the first time in 12 years to choose legislative representatives. It was, however, an exercise in limited democracy and was orchestrated by the military rulers. Only two parties, approved by the military, were allowed to enter candidates in the voting, which was the next to last phase in a return to civilian rule promised by the military. Presidential elections were scheduled for late 1992 and military officers said they would return authority to elected civilians in early 1993.

SOUTH AFRICA

The deeply divided Republic of South Africa, whose complex society is characterized by institutionalized racial discrimination known the world over as *apartheid,* has become a special kind of pariah in today's world. And yet South Africa had until recent years the best and freest press in all of Africa. However, it was (and is) a white man's press freedom.[5]

In this nation racked by sporadic violence and a simmering civil war, newspapers and broadcasting have been heavily involved in the strife and frictions which have evolved into a power struggle between two nationalisms—Afrikaner and African. As the violence has risen and positions have hardened, the press as both recorder and participant in the tragic drama has become increasingly muted and impotent.

South Africa's press historically has represented various constituent groups of this cellular society. The British settlers brought with them English language newspapers that reflected the values and functions of British newspapers. Backed by mining interests, commercially oriented, and serving the 2 million English speakers, several of these—the *Star* and *Rand Daily Mail* of Johannesburg, the *Argus* and *Cape Times* of Cape Town, for example—have been probably the best newspapers in Africa—outspoken, independent, and consistently opposed to apartheid and to the Afrikaner-dominated National Party that has ruled South Africa since 1948. (South Africa had no government newspapers nor did the Afrikaner viewpoint have the support of any English language paper until the *Citizen* was surreptitiously and illegally launched with government funding in 1976.)

But due to over 100 apartheid-related laws and other government pressures since 1948, the press's ability to report and criticize the government has steadily diminished. This decline of the general interest dailies had a clear benchmark, the closing in 1985 of the *Rand Daily Mail,* the most outspoken and courageous foe of apartheid of any newspaper in the world.

Following their defeat in the Boer War, the Afrikaners won their

struggle for political dominance in part through their Afrikaans language newspapers that faithfully supported, but rarely criticized,
the National Party. *Die Burger, Vaderland,* and more recently *Beeld*
and *Rapport* were the most prominent of the half dozen or so papers
of the 2.5 million Afrikaners. Closely allied to the National Party,
leading Afrikaner politicians such as H. F. Verwoerd and D. F. Malan
worked on these papers. In recent years, however, *Beeld,* the leading Afrikaans daily, has become increasingly critical of, and independent from, the Nationalists.

The third significant portion of South African journalism has
been the black press, at the cutting edge of confrontation between
black and white. This has been the most persecuted section of journalism because a government that denies full political rights to 84
percent of its citizens must of necessity repress any discussion of, or
call for, those rights. Consequently, the 23 million plus Africans, 2.7
million racially mixed Coloureds, and the 840,000 "Asians" have
over the years developed their own newspapers. Historians have
counted at least 800 publications put out by the nonwhite segments
of South Africa over the past 100 years.[6]

Since the Soweto uprising of 1976, the government has clearly
followed an escalating policy of repressing black political expression. A succession of black papers—including the highly popular
World and *Sunday World* in 1977 and their successors, *Post* and
Sunday Post, in 1981—were closed down by the Nationalists. Other
papers were intimidated, and black reporters have been singled out
for harassment, beatings, or detention without trial, hazards rarely
faced by their white colleagues. Except for the *City Press,* the *Sowe-
tan,* and a few church-supported publications, a black press barely
exists in South Africa. What little freedom of the press remains in
South Africa is a limited freedom of the white press to discuss white
politics.

Broadcasting, firmly under government control, contributes little to discussion of political alternatives or to full reporting of race
relations. The South African Broadcasting Corporation (SABC) is
the most pervasive and technically advanced radio and television
service in Africa. Its 16 radio services and 3 television channels
broadcast a total of 2,269 hours per week in 17 languages—impressive indeed by African standards. But SABC is disliked by hundreds
of thousands in all racial groups because it is completely controlled
by the Afrikaner elites who rule South Africa and adroitly manipulate broadcasting to help maintain political control.

The unprecedented violence centered in the African townships from 1984 to 1987 led to further restraints on free expression. State of Emergency regulations in effect dictated that in regard to black/white conflict, the press of South Africa can ONLY report what the South African government permits it to report. Foreign television and still cameras were barred from the townships and any scenes of unrest. During the two years after the nationwide State of Emergency was imposed, more than 800 people were killed and 20,000 were detained. The killing has continued. By late 1991, it was estimated that 11,000 people had been killed since 1984. Most had died as a result of black-on-black violence.

In sum, it should be emphasized that South Africa is the most highly industrialized nation of Africa, with a high living standard (enjoyed by about 20 percent of South Africans—mostly whites and a small fraction of nonwhites) that compares favorably with Western nations and with Singapore and Hong Kong. During the postwar economic development of the Republic, increasing numbers of white South Africans and significant numbers of urban blacks, Indians, and Coloureds have been reading newspapers and magazines, listening to radio, and watching movies, television, and video cassettes. As elsewhere in the West, media have been floating upward on the rising tide of economic development.

But since 1948, when the implementation of apartheid began, government censorship and repression of expression, to maintain white political and economic control, has steadily increased. Author Nadine Gordimer has said that censorship will not end until apartheid ends. And meaningful freedom of the press certainly will not return to South Africa until apartheid ends.

Though it has not ended, significant holes were carved into the solid apartheid structure in the late 1980s, and the opening years of the 1990s were a time of renewed hopes for most South Africans. The new leadership provided by President F. W. de Klerk showed it was willing to negotiate with the African majority and to try to deal with white South Africa's central problem: coming to terms with all the people of South Africa. The release of Nelson Mandela after 27 years in prison and the unbanning of the African National Congress changed the political atmosphere dramatically. Negotiations began with the ANC, and State of Emergency regulations were ended. Escalating violence between black factions unfortunately added a complicating element to the situation. Moreover, some apartheid laws were still in place and the African majority still had no vote, but there was a palpable feeling that the basic rules of political life were in the process of changing. Further, the press and broadcasting enjoyed much greater freedom to report all these dramatic events. The *Star's* stories about government death squads were particularly embarrassing to the security forces.

The gap left by the demise of the liberal *Rand Daily Mail* was filled to an extent by small "alternative" or anti-apartheid weeklies. Though under-financed and with small circulations, these outspoken journals reported much information not found in the mainstream media. The principal weeklies and their circulations were *Weekly Mail,* 30,000; *New Nation,* whose 70,000 readers were mostly Africans; *Vrye Weekblad,* an Afrikaans paper read by 10,000 Afrikaners; *South,* edited for 15,000 mixed-race Coloured readers; and *The Indicator,* with 30,000 distribution among the Indians, Africans, and Coloureds.

Although television and broadcasting were still government controlled, the SABC was more open and receptive to views and ideas it earlier suppressed or opposed. There also had been a clear easing of censorship of books and other publications. No one could be sure how long this new press freedom would last, and most agreed that South Africa still had a long way to go before achieving a just and democratic society. But for the first time in many years, there were reasons for optimism.

ROLE OF "EUROPEAN" NEWSPAPERS

From the perspective of the 1990s, the publications that have persisted and survived in African journalism, with a few exceptions, have been largely the newspapers with European roots and associations. This is true, certainly, of those in the three nations discussed above, the *Standard* and *Daily Nation* in Nairobi, the *Daily Times* and *Sunday Times* of Lagos, and the *Star* and *Sunday Times* of Johannesburg.

As was previously noted, the daily newspaper in Africa was (and is) essentially a European import or cultural transplant that came with the British, French, Portuguese, Italians, Germans, etc., in the nineteenth and early twentieth centuries. As a cultural artifact, the newspaper—whether as a government gazette, settler broadsheet, or African-oriented tabloid—spread along with other Western influences such as automobiles and roads, railroads, Christian churches and missions, schools, literacy in European languages, legal systems, and petty commerce.

These European papers prospered in those colonial administrative centers where the colonizers and settlers were most numerous and dominant—in Cape Town, Dakar, Nairobi, Abidjan, Salisbury (Harare), Johannesburg, Accra, Lagos, for example. Newspapers like *Dakar Matin, East African Standard, Daily Times, Daily Graphic, Rhodesian Herald, Rand Daily Mail,* and the *Star,* among others, were hothouse transplants in a few colonial enclaves. They provided the models in technology as well as format and content, delineating what a newspaper should be. For the few Africans involved in colonial times with journalism, these papers defined what journalism was about and how it should be practiced. Those influences persisted as more and more Africans practiced journalism.

Historically, the best and most influential newspapers as models or prototypes for African journalism were those in the British colonies that mainly served the British settlers or commercial interests.

The onetime Daily Mirror group papers—the *Daily Mail* in Freetown, the *Daily Graphic* in Accra, and the *Daily Times* in Lagos—had long since become government mouthpieces and propaganda sheets, but they still resembled, in form and style, their Fleet Street prototypes. Much the same impact was had by the East African Standard group of papers in Kenya, Tanzania, and Uganda, as well as the Argus papers of Rhodesia/Zimbabwe. These and other European papers provided a stimulating environment in which an African journalist could work and learn his trade. Over the years, many of Africa's best journalists, and there have been quite a number, learned what newspapering was all about from the European papers, either the ones they worked on or those brought in from overseas.

The numerous journalism training courses—such as the IPI Training Scheme in Nairobi, those of the Thomson Foundation, and various others in the United States, Britain, and France—reinforced these Western models of journalism. But it can be argued that, for West Africa certainly, the three London Mirror papers were a more influential and lasting school of journalism for African newsmen than the myriad training programs in and out of educational institutions.

The concepts of press freedom and other Western journalistic practices and ethics were internalized by these African journalists. African journalists, on and off the European papers, may have disagreed sharply with the politics of the *East African Standard,* the *Daily Times,* or the *Rhodesian Herald,* but these papers, as well as others, provided important models of what journalism could be and what freedom of the press was all about. These models and values are the products of Western liberal democracies.

The earlier generation of notable African journalists included the names of Peter Enahoro and Timothy Ulo Adebango of Nigeria, John Dumoga of Ghana, Kelvin Mlenga of Zambia, Hilary Ng'weno of Kenya, and Percy Qoboza of South Africa, to name just a few. As a mark of their excellence, all got into difficulties with their governments for editing outspoken independent newspapers. And the struggle between African journalists and their governments goes on. Almost every current issue of *Index on Censorship, IPI Report,* and *Committee to Protect Journalists Update* contains reports of recent actions by African governments to repress or jail journalists or to censor their publications. And today, given the great difficulties facing Africa, it can be argued that the best and most effective newspapers are those that have direct ties to earlier European publications or groups, such as the *Standard* and the *Nation* of Nairobi, the *Herald* and *Bulawayo Chronicle* of Zimbabwe, the *Times of Zambia* and *Zambian Mail* of Lusaka, the *Daily Times* of Nigeria, *Fraternité Matin* of Ivory Coast, and several South African papers, including the *Star, Cape Times, Cape Argus, Weekly Mail,* and *Sunday Times.*

All have been battered by the contemporary disaster of the African political economy and to a greater or lesser extent have become sycophantic or obeisant toward the ruling authorities. But they persist. In the technical sense alone, as daily newspapers they are superior to what else is around, and at least they hold the hope or potential what might yet be in African journalism.

EXTERNAL WESTERN MEDIA INFLUENCES

Because their own news media have been so inadequate, educated Africans have long relied on overseas media for news about themselves and Africa in general. Publications like *Le Monde, International Herald Tribune, Time, Newsweek,* and various British papers, such as the *Daily Telegraph, Financial Times,* and the *Economist,* are widely read. In addition, the international radio broadcasters (especially the BBC World Service, Radio France Internationale, Voice of America, and Deutsche Welle) have large audiences in Africa, particularly during times of crisis when local media either shut down or fail to report the news. These broadcasters, including Radio Moscow and Radio Beijing, also broadcast in major African languages—Swahili, Hausa, Somali, etc.—and provide information that cannot be easily censored, thus contributing in a significant way to the free flow of information. In international broadcasting, one man's news is another man's propaganda, and for Africans with shortwave radios, a good deal of both is available every evening.

Diversity of information is accessible in another way, because London and Paris have become the publishing centers for numerous magazines, newsletters, and weeklies specifically edited for African audiences. Many expatriate African journalists, forced out of journalism at home by politics, have helped produce such influential publications as *West Africa, Jeune Afrique, Drum, Africa Now, Africa Events, Afrique-Asie, Talking Drums,* among others, and the influential newsletters *Africa Confidential* and *African Research Bulletin.* The quality of this journalism has been enhanced by such able journalists as Peter Enahoro (*Africa Now*), Ralph Uwueche (*Africa*), and Cameron Doudu and Elizabeth Ohene (*Talking Drums*). A big advantage of Paris- or London-based publication is freedom from censorship and political pressures. Over a quarter century after the end of colonial rule, the two major colonial capitals are still, for economic as well as political reasons, the best places to publish quality *African* journalism.

SUMMARY: WHY THE FALSE START

As the foregoing discussion has indicated, newspapers failed to grow and prosper in Africa after colonialism for a variety of reasons. Let me recapitulate what I consider to be the primary causes, some of which surely overlap with others.

First, the newly independent one-party governments during the 1960s were hostile to newspapers or publications they could not control. Even the small African papers that led the fight against colonialism became enemies of the new class that ruled Africa. European papers were particularly suspect, and many were either closed down or converted into government papers. *African* journalists, whether in Nigeria, Kenya, Cameroon, Ghana, Uganda, or South Africa, were systematically persecuted and harassed by the politicians who controlled the destinies of the fragile new states.

As a result, government control of the press has stunted African journalism and this has usually resulted in dull, obeisant, and uninformative newspapers. Official newspapers failed to provide useful, informative news coverage and incisive discussion and criticism of public affairs. Government/party papers in Ghana under Nkrumah and his military successors, Nyerere's Tanzania, and Kaunda's Zambia, to cite several examples, have uniformly been sleepwalking automatons bearing little resemblance to the lively papers that preceded them.

Africa's arbitrary and authoritarian regimes have prevented Africa's newspapers from playing a vital role in public affairs. Despite the controls and restraints they contended with under colonial rule, African newspapers at that time were free enough to be advocates of special interests or causes: the *East African Standard* espousing claims of British settlers against the aroused Kikuyus; the *Star* arguing for British mining interests against the Boer Republic in the Transvaal; Azikiwe's *West African Pilot,* the *Kumasi Pioneer,* and similar papers demanding independence for West Africans from British rule; and so on. But today's kept press has had little impact on public affairs, much less on economic development or political integration.

Second, economic and social conditions in Africa have not been favorable for expanding an informed and interested reading public. Newspaper readership has remained confined to the capitals and a few large cities where the few educated Africans, employed in either government or urban occupations, resided.

Due to illiteracy, poverty, malnutrition, and linguistic diversity, the majority of Africans—peasants living on subsistence agriculture and many others crowded into urban slums—remain untouched by the printed word. Newspapers remain "European" in that they are elite institutions speaking to that minority who live in cities, are educated, are literate, and generally run the government or are involved in the small modern sector. This is obviously an important audience but it is not the broad public, and hence newspapers continue as an elite, not a mass, medium.

The absence of general economic development is a prime reason for failure of media systems to develop as they have in India, Singapore, and Hong Kong. Also, of course, there has been the lack of a literate and prosperous public to support and use the media. The only exception is South Africa, which has been blighted by the scourge of apartheid.

Third, the economic and social conditions necessary for newspapers and other publications to survive as commercial enterprises have been in short supply. Dearth of capital and foreign investment, entrepreneurs, available and affordable presses and printing equipment, and the trained people to publish newspapers have been generally lacking except in a few urban centers such as Nairobi, Lagos, Dakar, Abidjan, Harare, and those of South Africa. For an independent press to survive and profit financially, it must be anchored in a robust economy that generally is separate and distinct from the political regime. This, with a few exceptions, Africa has lacked. As commercial enterprises, African media usually are not profitable. In free market societies, the economic realm where the media are located is generally clearly separated from the political realm. But in socialist nations with centralized planning, as economist Robert Heilbroner points out, the economic and political realms tend to overlap to a great extent. Hence, the economy and the media are subject to political control.[7] This has been the usual experience in Africa's one-party states.

Except in Nigeria and South Africa, newspapers have not been widely distributed beyond the city of publication because of transport and road problems. Newspaper circulation is kept down, as well, by the high cost of imported newsprint, which is often rationed by governments for political reasons, i.e., newspapers that annoy the government may be denied newsprint. In television, African broadcasters, aside from South Africa, have not adequately developed their own programs and films as has happened in Hong Kong and Singapore. Instead, they have relied on Western imports.

Fourth, constitutional and legal difficulties have thwarted privately owned papers. Without rule of law, especially legal protection for civil liberties and private property—and for minority rights—little hope for a free and vigorous press exists. Without legal protection and a stable government, media usually founder.

All across the continent, from Kenya to Ghana to Zimbabwe, there is little legal protection for minority viewpoints; all were expected to "get on board" and support the government in power whether elected or the result of a military takeover. Without a legal opposition (and there usually is not one) and the right of individual citizens to criticize their governors, the press itself has little freedom to express displeasure or criticism of the regime.

Fifth, Africa's disastrous slide into penury—which has affected even the comparatively successful states of the Ivory Coast, Cameroon, Kenya, and South Africa—has further aggravated the economic conditions needed for newspapers and other media to take root and grow. In mass communication, as in most other aspects of modernity, Africa is slipping further and further behind the rest of the world.

Finally, in looking around the world, it is apparent that newspapers have done best in open, democratic societies with high average incomes and free market economies, in countries where there are two distinct regimes: one economic devoted to making money and one political that governs the nation. In most African countries, whether run by socialists or soldiers, political rulers dominate the economy.

Effective newspapers, anchored in the private sector, that serve their readers by providing accurate and meaningful news and intelligent commentary on public affairs are few and far between in Africa. The few that approach these standards are in a few neo-colonial and free market centers. Private ownership, European models of journalism, foreign investment and expertise all appear to be important factors in producing these few viable newspapers. Only South Africa has approached a media system comparable to that of Western nations and on a par with what developed in several Asian nations during the past generation.

Two highly significant recent trends in Africa—the widespread rejection of one-party government and the demise of centralized socialist economic controls—portend important changes in the news media as well. Throughout the sub-Sahara in 1991, ordinary Africans had been confronting dictators at revolutionary "national conferences" to demand multiparty democracy. Sixteen one-party states have legalized opposition parties in response to democracy movements and three Marxist governments were unseated by the ballot box—in Benin, Cape Verde, and Sao Tome and Principe.

President Kenneth Kaunda of Zambia, one of Africa's longest serving rulers, was resoundingly defeated in a multiparty election—the first such contest in Zambia in over decades. This sent shock waves to every major one-party state, from Ivory Coast to Zaire to Kenya to Malawi to Zimbabwe, putting them under increasing pressures to democratize their political systems and to permit more political parties.

More open and diverse political systems will certainly provide a more hospitable setting climate for independent news media. But significant growth and improvement in Africa's mass media may be slow in coming because of Africa's long-term economic and social problems.

II

ASIAN SUCCESS STORIES

To broaden our perspective of Third World media beyond the African scene, we visited India, Singapore, and Hong Kong to investigate the role that the mass media play in the public life of these three Asian societies.

The central research question was: Why have the media flourished and their audiences expanded so in the Indian subcontinent and these two small city-states? What are the factors—economic, social, political, cultural, ideological—that seem to have contributed to the growth of sophisticated media systems that stand out in such marked contrast to those of the anglophone nations of Africa with whom they share a similar colonial history?

A second, but not secondary, purpose was to look at press and government relationships. How free or independent of government controls are the media of India, Singapore, and Hong Kong, and what role if any do independent newspapers and broadcast media play in national affairs and public opinion?

Here, then, are case studies of three rare successes of economic and media development in the Third World. Surprisingly, the literature on communication and devel-

opment neglects the successes of the two island city-states and only recently recognizes the accomplishments of India. Hong Kong, in particular, with its colonial status (which ends in 1997 when possession reverts to the People's Republic of China), economic freedom, and lack of foreign aid and centralized planning, seems to have defied the conventional wisdom about how development—and media growth—occurs.

Along with Singapore, these two "jewels in the crown" of the British Commonwealth have in some ways outpaced their former and current British masters and have benefited greatly from foreign investment and unrestricted trade with the capitalistic West, especially the United States and Japan. (India has tended to restrict foreign investment and trade but has prospered in part because of development of its huge domestic markets. Economists have advised that India would benefit from more foreign trade.)

Moreover, this study is predicated on the notion that a revision or rethinking about the interplay of mass communications and economic development is needed. The failures both of foreign aid to make a significant difference in economic growth and of centralized, socialist states (as in much of Africa) to manage their economies effectively have contributed to this phenomenon. Further, the roles of personal incentives, of free enterprise and market economies, and of multinational corporations to stimulate growth in Third World nations are now being viewed as far more central to development than was previously thought to be the case. The spectacular economic growth of the "Four Tigers" (South Korea, Taiwan, Hong Kong, and Singapore) in recent years has contributed greatly, of course, to this changed perspective.

It can be argued that Singapore and Hong Kong are now essentially First World nations so complete has their modernization been in the past generation. But that was not the case as recently as 25 years ago.

Much about Hong Kong and Singapore is different from other new nations; both are small offshore states which lack large numbers of rural peasants, both are highly urbanized, and both are dominated by overseas Chinese.

Singapore, under the highly competent and paternalistic (some say authoritarian) rule of Lee Kuan Yew, the only prime minister the island republic had known until 1991, has had special circumstances as well. Singapore's economic miracle has been similar to Hong Kong's, but the model has been different. State or corporate capitalism ("Singapore, Inc."), with direct government planning and involvement in economic activities and clear policies to encourage foreign investment and trading, is the name of the game. Hong Kong and Singapore live and die by free trade, and until recently, they have both been living quite well. (These economies differ clearly from the parastatal corporatism of African states, which are often characterized by inefficiency, centralized planning, and corruption and are not tied in to foreign trade.)

Singapore's media and their audiences are on a par with those of Hong Kong, with one important difference. Singapore's public communication is thoroughly controlled, and the press in particular is subject to the arbitrary and, at times, ruthless interference by Lee Kuan Yew himself.

Hong Kong and Singapore are certainly special cases, but yet I believe that study of the factors that have contributed to mass communication development there can prove useful in understanding why the media have not developed in most of Africa.

Perhaps more direct comparisons with the media of anglophone Africa can be made by looking first at India, which shares so many characteristics with Africa: burgeoning populations, linguistic and ethnic diversity, communal strife and enmity, competing religions, and many millions of impoverished rural peoples.

6

INDIA: A FREE PRESS SURVIVES

In Africa, it has been said that a free press has never really been tried (except perhaps in South Africa). In independent India, a free press has not only been tried but has persisted for over 40 years, much to the amazement of many Indians as well as friends of India.

As the world's largest democracy and the second largest nation, India's free press has played a crucial, if abrasive, role in that great experiment. Indian democracy is remarkable for the amount of freedom of communication it permits its citizens. Indians can and do freely organize political parties, trade unions, chambers of commerce, student and civic groups, and caste, religious, and ethnic assocations.

Despite occasional clashes with politicians, Indian newspapers and publications are generally free from government interference and are multiplying in numbers and circulations in all the languages. Much of the press speaks out on public affairs and has been critical of its prime ministers. Radio and television, however, are government owned and controlled, and thus lack credibility in public affairs.

The recent explosive growth in mass communication is related to the industrial boom that has brought comparative affluence and increased consumer goods, including television sets and VCRs, to the expanding middle class. The impressive expansion of Indian mass media in the postcolonial period, while still maintaining press freedom, stands out in marked contrast to the media stagnation of anglophone Africa.

Yet India has been, and continues to be, a deeply troubled and problem-ridden sea of humanity. V. S. Naipaul called it a "wounded civilization," and John K. Galbraith referred to it as a "functioning anarchy." In 1989, India was trying to cope with such grave problems as corruption in Prime Minister Rajiv Gandhi's ruling government, birth control, terrorism in Punjab and Assam, revolt of local landowners in various regions, Hindu-Muslim riots, violence of the Gurkhas in West Bengal, involvement of Indian troops in the ethnic conflict in Sri Lanka, and a possible nuclear threat from Pakistan.[1]

In 1991, the nation was severely shaken by the assassination of Prime Minister Rajiv Gandhi; the economy seemed to be collapsing, sectarian conflicts were widespread, and there was talk of national disintegration. But under the new prime minister, P. V. Narasimha Rao, a new and more hopeful political era seemed to be beginning. In short order, the new leader abandoned the rickety socialist economic structure left to him by the Gandhis and declared that foreign investors were welcome. Many problems remain, including a full-scale separatist insurgency in a Kashmir valley, where 4 million Muslims live.

Further, any perceptive visitor to India can see as well that there is much that is deficient and troubling about the press and broadcasting. Free newspapers are not necessarily good ones. But India's problems are not hidden away; they are out front for one and all to see. The press corps, foreign and domestic, is free to roam the vast subcontinent of 3,287,263 square kilometers and report what it sees. There are no secret gulags or large areas closed to travelers and journalists as in China.

COMPARISONS WITH AFRICA

India and Africa share similar Third World characteristics. Both are large regions with heterogeneous and diverse peoples, numerous languages, and conflicting religions, all marked by deep historic cleavages and communal strife. The main languages, as indicated by millions of speakers, are Hindi, 163; Telegu, 45; Bengali, 45; Marathi, 42; Tamil, 38; Urdu, 29; Gujarati, 26; Malayalam, 22; Kannada, 22; and Oriya, 20.[2] These principal languages separate the major regions, and within each linguistic region, there are vast dialect variations. Hindi, the official language, is spoken by only a fraction of Indians and is heard mostly in the north. Bombay residents claim 222 mother tongues and 24 linguistic groups of 1,000 or more are found in that one city.

English, though spoken by only about 50 million, is important as a link language, connecting many educated Indians from different regions with different mother tongues. These English speakers support nearly two dozen news and business magazines (half of which started in the mid-1980s) plus a dozen major newspapers, including some of the great dailies inherited from the British Raj, such as *Times of India*, the *Statesman*, the *Hindu*, and the *Tribune*.

Religions, as well, separate people. The main faiths practiced, in millions of adherents, are Hinduism, 550; Islam, 76; Christianity, 16; Sikhism, 13; Buddhism, 5; and Jainism, 3.[3]

In addition to language and religion, Indians are divided as well by caste and socioeconomic classes. About 35 percent of the nearly 850 million Indians live in abject poverty, but due to recent economic gains, another 350 to 400 million Indians have standards of living ranging from adequate to lavish.

But as in much of Africa, India must cope with a relentlessly expanding population that negates many social and economic gains, making it difficult to cope with poverty and disease. Fifty thousand babies are born every day. Population projections indicate that by 2010, India will become the world's most populous nation with 1.63 billion people, compared with China's 1.54 billion people.

Considering India's larger population, it is accurate to say that India has a broader cultural base than Africa—more educated people, more doctors, more engineers and scientists. In fact, India claims both to have the world's third largest concentration of scientists, next only to the United States and the Soviet Union, and to be the tenth most industrialized nation on earth. Certainly the progress India has made in satellite communication would not have been possible without impressive scientific and industrial resources.

This scientific and technological development must be related to India's impressive expansion of education. In 1951, India had 28 universities, 147 professional colleges, and 547 arts/sciences colleges, with a total enrollment of 174,000. By 1985, there were 135 universities, 1,500 professional colleges, and 3,500 arts/sciences colleges showing a twentyfold increase in enrollment to 3,442,000 students.[4]

In contrast, most of Africa has lagged badly in education. Although the new African nations gave high priority to expanded educational opportunities, schools and universities of anglophone Africa have not expanded in comparable fashion.

Another impressive indicator of Indian development is its 61,640 kilometers of railways, which daily carry over 9 million passengers and .75 million tons of freight. Track mileage and routes have expanded considerabaly since independence. African railways (generally unimproved since colonial times) cannot begin to compare with India's more than 10,000 locomotives, 40,000 coaches, and 400,000 freight cars. India's modernization in both agriculture and industry has ridden on the railroads. At the peak harvest season, nearly 100 freight trains with 100 cars each day leave the Punjab, the heart of India's green revolution.[5]

SIMILAR COLONIAL HISTORY

The British ruled India much longer than they did their African colonies, though both regions were subjected to similar influences: British trade and commerce, British law, and the traditions and practices of British journalism, including the legal and professional concepts of freedom of the press and independent journalism as a kind of Fourth Estate. Elites from both regions pursued higher education in the United Kingdom.

Under the British Raj, British newspapers had a much longer time in which to sink their roots. Printing technology, including moveable type, came from Europe three centuries ago. The first daily newspaper was printed in 1790, in English, when James Augustus Hicky started the *Bengal Gazette*. India's great English language papers of today go back to the 19th century. The *Times of India* began as an English weekly in 1838 and became a daily in 1850; it remains India's biggest daily. The *Statesman* was started in 1875 and the *Hindu* in 1878. The *Tribune* celebrated its 100th anniversary in 1981. Vernacular papers had an early start as well; *Bombay Samachar*, a daily in Gujarati, was founded in 1822 and is the oldest local language paper.

The powerful force of nationalism contributed to the growth of the press in both regions. Mohandas Gandhi and Jawaharlal Nehru, the founding fathers of modern India, both wrote for or started newspapers to oppose British rule and to urge independence. Gandhi, who had earlier started *Indian Opinion* in South Africa in 1903, founded two weeklies in India, *Young India* in 1919 and *Harijan* in

1933. Nehru became chairman of the board of directors of the *National Herald* in 1938.

As mentioned in chapter 2, African nationalists such as Azikiwe, Kenyatta, Nkrumah, Kaunda, Awolowo, and others in colonial British Africa started and edited newspapers to aid their political parties and nationalist goals.

Yet, during the first years of independence, the newspapers of India and anglophone Africa took divergent paths. The English language papers of India after 1947 were acquired from British owners by Indian capitalists and became completely Indianized while retaining the practices and traditions of British journalism, including a strong feeling for freedom of the press. This was respected by law and grudgingly accepted by the political leadership.

In anglophone Africa, on the other hand, such a complete cultural transfer did not take place. The British-owned papers were either bought out and made into government papers, as happened in Ghana, Nigeria, Sierra Leone, Tanzania, Zambia, and Zimbabwe, or they were subjected to harsh government restrictions and pressures, as in Kenya and South Africa. The new African governments did not tolerate or protect them by law as independent critical voices in public affairs. Hence, today India has a free press; Africa has a kept or controlled press.

Another crucial difference between India and Africa relates to national boundaries. The British left India in 1947 (after the partitioning off of Pakistan, which Britain opposed) as a whole country, one nation for better or worse. But Africa at independence in the early 1960s was left as a maze of 40-odd countries, with the same borders that were illogically drawn at the 1885 Berlin conference.

Thus, India, despite its diversity and complexity, has had the critical mass necessary to develop a truly national mass media system. National newspapers and magazines and nationwide radio and television broadcasting (augmented by the Insat I-B communication satellite system) became possible and, in time, jumped over linguistic and cultural barriers. Furthermore, numerous regional newspapers, based on vernacular languages, have flourished in India.

By contrast, African media systems, except for Nigeria and South Africa, have long been hemmed in by their confining borders, which have severely limited their potential growth. The English/French linguistic split in West and Central Africa, for example, limits the reach of media. African newspapers tend to be restricted to the capital and urban centers of small nations, but the

Times of India, Hindu, Statesman, and *Indian Express* are each available daily in the great cities of India—Delhi, Bombay, Madras, and Calcutta.

India's political unity has been crucial as well for the vast internal market it provides for the impressive industrial expansion of recent years. Rajiv Gandhi's main accomplishment, according to Ved Mehta, was the loosening of government economic controls, "which has released a potent, almost explosive energy, and perhaps set the stage for a new era of private industry and a new generation of entrepreneurs."[6]

Despite its socialist beginnings, India has moved increasingly toward private enterprise. In 1991, the minister of finance said the nation now looks to South Korea and prosperous Southeast Asian nations as guiding economic symbols. He said India hoped to attract multinational corporations to look upon India for investments and profitable investments. For its first four decades, India had been suspicious of capitalism, the United States, foreign investment, and trade. Now that is clearly changing. This has greatly aided India's consumer economy, which in turn has fueled media growth in new publications and more sales of television sets and VCRs. Some 100 million Indians are estimated to be participating in the consumer boom. "One product that is consumed by a large part of this group, despite India's 60 percent illiteracy, is the printed word. Newspapers and magazines are a dynamic growth industry, crammed with advertisements for the good life."[7]

Africa, except for South Africa, has gone through no comparable industrialization and economic expansion.

PRESS FREEDOM

India started its political independence in 1947 with a democracy and a free press, and despite its ups and downs, it has managed to hold onto both. The press's freedom is protected by law, and that freedom to speak out on public affairs is a key reason why democracy has managed to survive.

New African nations began their independence with ostensibly democratic governments, but most soon gave way to authoritarian one-party regimes that controlled public communication. In Africa, press freedom did not long survive political independence and mostly has not been protected by law. As noted before, African journalists and their newspapers have often been victimized by arbitrary regimes. But as a value, press freedom survives among African journalists and a few lawyers, academics, and others in Africa.

The Indian press has serious shortcomings. Indian newspapers sometimes lend themselves to government manipulation and are subject to pressures from official advertisers and suppliers of newsprint. The press generally is not noted for investigative reporting and neglects important areas of news coverage. One critic says the press prefers to discuss rumors or gossip instead of facts or hard news, and often after an initial story of some import, there will be no follow-up stories. But India's press is still unfettered, and some papers have not been reluctant to criticize, even excoriate, its prime ministers.

The greatest confrontation between the press and government occurred in 1975–77, when Prime Minister Indira Gandhi declared a state of emergency, a 20-month period marked by clear censorship. Political opponents, including some journalists, were jailed, and few newspapers, with the notable exception of the *Indian Express,* spoke out in protest. However, when Mrs. Gandhi put her policies to the test of a national election, she was soundly defeated, and democracy *with* press freedom returned to the subcontinent.

The acerbic, uneasy, and confrontational relationship between India's government and press has continued unabated. In 1988, the press came under its worst attack since 1975–77, when the lower house of parliament passed a tough defamation bill prescribing a mandatory jail term for offending journalists. The bill came at a time when newspapers and magazines had been publishing frequent reports of corruption and misuse of power by officials in the Rajiv Gandhi government. After widespread protests by journalists and opposition politicians, the bill was withdrawn.[8] Earlier, in 1987, the *Indian Express,* the arch media foe of Gandhi, came under direct (and some thought illegal) pressure from the government. Authorities took advantage of an industrial dispute at the New Delhi edition of the daily, alleged various infractions of import regulations, harassed, and, in effect, shut down the paper for a time. The *Express,* however, survived.[9]

GROWTH OF INDIAN MEDIA

Over a period of many years now, a clear pattern of media growth in India has developed—a pattern that seems related to both an expanding economy and a free and open communication system. This growth has occurred, despite being stymied at times by government policies; for years, Indian governments resisted the introduction of television and thwarted the expansion of broadcasting by heavy-handed government controls of All India Radio and television. Controls on newsprint, which is expensive and paid for by hard currency, had restricted circulation growth of publications.

Yet the long-term growth of the press has been impressive. In 1950, there were 214 daily newspapers—44 in English and the rest in 13 Indian languages, principally Hindi (44), Urdu (44), Gujerati (17), and Marathi (17).[10] By 1987, India had 1,500 daily newspapers and 22,000 other publications printed in more than 90 regional languages and dialects.

The total number of newspapers and periodicals has grown more than three times from the late 1950s to the early 1980s. The consumption of newsprint increased from 77,782 tons in 1957–58 to more than 350,000 tons in 1985.[11] Although the major national dailies and newsmagazines were in English, the impressive recent growth of the Indian press has been in regional vernacular language publications. In 1954, total circulation of dailies was 2.5 million copies; currently it is over 15 million.[12]

Each great city of India has its own English-language daily. For Delhi, it is the *Hindustan Times;* Bombay, *Times of India;* Madras, the *Hindu;* Bangalore, *Deccan Herald;* and Calcutta, the *Statesman.* The *Indian Express,* which has 10 editions, is not identified with any one of these cities but circulates in all of them. As mentioned, these national dailies are each available in other major cities as well. The *Times of India,* with 650,000 circulation (325,000 in Bombay alone), is the biggest press organization, putting out 19 other publications as well.

The *Indian Express,* with over 700,000 circulation, is more outspoken and carries more hard news. The *Hindu,* the leader in new technology, uses facsimile with the Insat I-B satellite to distribute its regional editions and has adopted offset printing, phototypesetting, and utilizes a fleet of DC-5 airplanes to distribute papers around India.

The daily press, however, is considered by some as rather stodgy and set in its ways. The new vigor in Indian journalism has come from the large number of weekly newsmagazines which appeared after the Emergency of 1975–77 and were largely a reaction against the more docile daily papers. The newsmagazines ignore the taboos of the older dailies and are attracting a new breed of bright, young, aggressive journalists. Best known is *India Today,* a copycat of *Time*, which also has an edition in Hindi. Others are *Frontline, Imprint* (a monthly), *Sunday*, and *Illustrated Weekly*.

The vernacular papers often do good reporting but are more provincial and narrow in their coverage, speaking for regional interests or ethnic/linguistic groups. The English papers focus on national concerns and serve the big city elites; the Hindi papers only go to the northern Hindi belt, but the vernacular papers serve their regions well. For example, Malayalam papers reach every corner of thickly populated Kerala state. Professor Eapen said it is customary for Kerala homes to subscribe to a specialized publication such as a women's magazine as well as a general newspaper, both in Malayalam. One popular Malayalam weekly in Kerala state has a circulation of 1.5 million.[13]

Television has been coming on strong recently, and as a result, newspapers and magazines are losing advertising revenue to the little box. Radio and television are under government control and reflect the "protocol news" found as well on many African broadcast services. The half hour evening television news shows are dominated by the daily activities of the prime minister, no matter how trival, whether signing agreements, welcoming a foreign visitor, etc. Any significant world news is squeezed in at the end. Further, broadcast news reflects government policy; during the war in Afghanistan, the news was told only from the Soviet point of view, since India was then diplomatically close to Moscow.

The advent of the Insat I-B satellite, placed in orbit in August 1983 by the U.S. shuttle *Challenger*, has made possible nationwide and direct television broadcasting. Credit goes to Indian scientists who developed the Indian National Satellite (Insat) at a cost of $130 million. The cost of developing a comparable land-based telecommunication system in the subcontinent was estimated at $1 trillion. Not only does Insat provide direct broadcasting to some 25,000 television sets in rural villages, it also monitors weather on the subcontinent and provides computerized linkages for transport, tourism, and other nationwide communications.

But the real boom in electronic communication is occurring in the cities, where videocassettes and movies are joining in. India has long been a major film producer of the world, turning out over 700 feature films a year, mainly at the Indian "Hollywood," Bombay. Many of those films are now finding their way onto television screens, either by broadcast or videocassettes, and of course are very popular. In the mid-1980s, the government was opening television transmitters at the rate of one a day, and it was expected that

70 percent of the population would soon be in the reach of broadcasting originating in New Delhi and other big cities by way of Insat I-B.

With a budget of over $700 million annually for five years (beginning in 1988), Indian officials are claiming that their television network, with 417 transmitters, will be the largest in the world. In 1988, there were 80 million viewers and 11 million television set owners. Set owners are increasing at the rate of 1 million annually.[14]

Doordarshan (which means "distant vision" in Hindi), the government-owned television network, has moved into production of its own soap operas. In 1988, Doordarshan had only 13 full production centers but after five years expected to have 48.[15] Television is criticized as being too urban oriented since only 100 million live in cities, while most Indians live in the 500,000 villages. Further, critics say that programs produced by the single, government-owned network are shoddy, unprofessional, and downright dull.[16] And for a people who value free expression, much of the government-controlled television news is considered to be biased. Nevertheless, television sets are proliferating, and aerials can be seen sprouting out of modest village homes all over the country. A television drama series depicting the Hindu epic *Ramayana* attracted great interest in 1988, and television critics estimated that more than 100 million people watched the show each Sunday morning.

During the Gulf War in 1990–91, satellite television broadcasting arrived in India as satellite dishes appeared on the rooftops of New Delhi, Bombay, Calcutta, and Madras as well as countless other cities and communities as Indians watched uncensored television for the first time. During the Persian Gulf War and Moscow coup attempt, urban India was swept up in watching the Cable News Network, which has become so important in international broadcast news. Later, MTV and the BBC's new World Service Television, a mixture of news and entertainment, were added to the menu. All of this was possible because of AsiaSat, a satellite now positioned over Asia and available to broadcasters who wish to reach an audience of nearly 3 billion people. Programs are beamed up and down by way of the Hong Kong–based Star TV. For India this means that the longtime government monopoly over broadcasting has been broken, and India has become a much more open society as a result.

CONCLUSIONS

Since independence in 1947, India's free press has played a crucial role in the survival of India's fragile democracy, which would have been impossible without such openness. Flawed though they both are, parliamentary democracy and the press have shown a remarkable persistence in the face of overwhelming problems.

Further, it is apparent that the impressive expansion of both print and broadcasting media in recent years is related to the expanding free market economy of India. The growing boom in consumer goods has certainly aided media growth, especially through sales of advertising, television sets, videocassette recorders, and publications of all kinds. So, here again is evidence of a media system "floating upward on a rising tide of economic development."

This impressive media growth has been facilitated by the free and open political atmosphere of Indian public life. This open ambiance has stimulated the entrepreneurial spirit among publishers and editors throughout what Charles de Gaulle called "a dust of humanity."

The future of India is uncertain and clouded. Beset by deep and divisive problems, it has defied experts who a dozen years ago had written India off as a failed nation. But whatever happens, communication media will undoubtedly continue to play a central role in bridging the deep chasms between India's labyrinth of diverse and antagonistic communities.

7

SINGAPORE: MEDIA DEVELOPMENT WITHOUT PRESS FREEDOM

The Pacific Rim nations of Singapore, Hong Kong, South Korea, and Taiwan have enjoyed spectacular economic growth during the past generation. In each of these "Four Tigers," the mass media have expanded and audiences proliferated as people of these nations achieved higher incomes, better education and literacy, and increased leisure time.

Twenty-five years ago, all four were clearly Third World nations, with all the shortcomings and difficulties that expression conveys; today, these prospering nations, and their media systems, share many attributes of the First World.

Singapore is a rare success story in media development, but one that has been achieved without press freedom. We will examine why mass communication has flourished there while media have foundered or regressed in numerous other nations around the world that received political independence about the same time.

Admittedly, Singapore is a special case which shares few of the problems of the Third World, mainly because it is a small city-state without multitudes of rural peasants. Yet, considered as a case study, Singapore's experience perhaps can tell us something useful about mass communication and development.[1] This tiny city-state of only 2.6 million people crowded onto an island of only 588 square kilometers at the tip of the Malay Peninsula is one of the most dramatic examples of economic development in the postwar world. In less than a generation, this collection of poor, fractured, and contentious communities of Chinese, Indians, and Malays has evolved into a prosperous society that is highly educated, well fed and well housed, gainfully employed, and enjoying a per capita income of over $7,000, the highest in Asia after Japan. Singapore is orderly, clean, beautifully landscaped, and (some would say) dull. Economic success since the early 1970s has turned the country into an efficient, corruption-free country where telephones work, streets are safe, air is clean, and the water is pure. Chinese speaking a variety of dialects are 77 percent of the population, Malays 15 percent, and Indians 6 percent. In this polyglot society, English and Mandarin dominate as media languages.

Singapore was founded in 1819 by Sir Stamford Raffles as a commercial and trading center, and the island was under the rule of the British Raj from India until 1867 when it became a crown colony administered from London. After World War II, Singapore and Malaysia gained independence as a federation, but in 1965, Singapore separated from the mainland country, becoming an independent republic. Singapore has been ruled in an autocratic manner since 1959 by Lee Kuan Yew and his People's Action Party (PAP). Lee stepped aside in 1991 in favor of his protege, Goh Chok Tong, but Lee still heads the party and retains considerable power. During the turbulent sixties, Prime Minister Lee's main problems were the Communists, race riots, and an impoverished country. Lee's "soft authoritarianism," as it has been called, subdued his main opposition—the Communist-infiltrated labor unions, the universities, and the domestic press. The brilliant and combative Lee has never been willing to brook political opposition.

While Lee maintained rigid authoritarian control in the political sphere, he allowed a large amount of freedom in the city-state's economic sector, which has made spectacular gains under his free trade policies. Thus, Singapore has not followed the liberal model of national development but that of a corporate state with government managing the economy while attracting multinational corporations and developing free trade opportunities. This government-guided economy—"Singapore, Incorporated"—has produced impressive results and effectively tied itself to the growing Asian economy.[2] As the only prime minister Singapore has ever known, Lee is the CEO of Singapore, Inc., and has personally intervened in most aspects of Singaporean life,[3] especially the press.

TAMING THE SINGAPORE PRESS

From the beginning, Lee has played an active role in shaping and firmly controlling mass media. In May 1971, Lee acted against three private newspapers critical of his policies by forcing the closure of two English language dailies, *Eastern Sun* and the *Singapore Herald*, and by detaining four senior executives of the *Nyang Siang Pau*, a Chinese language paper. The *Eastern Sun* was accused of being a fifth column Communist newspaper backed by Hong Kong Communist sources. The *Singapore Herald* was accused of "taking on" the government by eroding the will and attitudes of the people over national service, agitating over labor laws, and advocating permissiveness in sex, drugs, and dress styles. The *Nyang Siang Pau* was accused of a deliberate effort to stir up Chinese racial emotions.[4]

In 1982, Lee again cracked down on the press in order to neutralize his political challengers. The government harshly criticized several editors and pressured them to stop covering the tiny political opposition, which had only one member in parliament. Lee also named his former director of national intelligence to oversee the *Straits Times*, the leading English language paper, and ordered the Straits Times Group to relinquish its afternoon paper, the *New Nation*, for a nominal fee and to turn it over to a rival company. These developments met with almost no public protest.[5]

Lee has long placed stringent limits on public discussion of political issues and has moved ruthlessly against any perceived political or press opponents. As a result of the earlier political wars, insecurity, if not paranoia, has characterized Lee's government. Tiny Singapore, in Lee's view, is surrounded by hostile and threatening neighbors of differing religions and ethnic origins, i.e., the Malaysians and Indonesians, many of whom are Moslems.

IMPRESSIVE MEDIA GROWTH

Lee Kuan Yew has attained his objective of "taming" the domestic press of Singapore. And yet, despite the repressive political atmosphere, the press and broadcasting have expanded and consumption of mass communication has become an increasingly important pastime in Singapore during the past 20 years. Clearly, this trend is related to Singapore's growing economy and rising per capita income, as well as improved education and literacy.

The growth of literacy has paralleled media growth. Since 1969, the ability to read has climbed at the rate of 1 percent per year to over 86 percent. Over half the people speak English, although Chinese is preferred by most Chinese. Forty-seven percent of all adults read Chinese newspapers, while 43 percent of adults read English papers. In all, 84 percent read a daily newspaper, which is high indeed and is 6 percent more than the number who watched television in 1987.

Media growth, however, has been accompanied by media consolidation. In 1980, 12 daily newspapers were published, with a 13th expected in 1981. Of the 12, 3 were in English, 5 in Chinese, 1 in Malay, 2 in Tamil, and 1 in Malayalam. The total daily circulation in 1979 was reported as 587,000, giving a circulation rate of 269 papers per 1,000 people. This was a healthy growth from a rate of about 200 per 1,000 in 1974.[6]

Only 6 dailies remained in 1988: 2 in English, 3 in Chinese, and 1 small daily in 'Tamil. But circulation penetration was impressive: *Straits Times,* with a staff of about 277, had a circulation of 269,108 and reached 600,000 people, while its stablemate, *Business Times,* with 66 staffers, reached a much smaller, more specialized readership of 15,000.[7]

The 2 major Chinese newspapers, *Lianhe Zaobao* and *Wanbao,* had a combined circulation of 264,000, and according to Survey Research of Singapore, 980,000 people read one of these Chinese papers out of 1.1 million people literate in the language.[8]

With a bilingual educational system, many Singaporeans read both English and Chinese publications. The prime minister has encouraged the use of English as an integrative language, and the rising educated middle class has taken advantage of the 3,700 publications imported onto the island. Some publications and books, especially any favorable to Communism or critical of Lee, are prohibited; still, the variety of reading matter available at newsstands and bookstores is impressive.

However, all five major dailies are published by the same conglomerate, Singapore Press Holdings, which is very much under the influence of, and at times direct interference by, Lee Kuan Yew. Simply put, this means that no daily newspaper will print anything that offends the government. If a paper does, then editors are fired and replaced by others more in accord with Lee's views at that time. Peter Lim, editor in chief of the four Straits Times Press newspapers (a subsidiary of Singapore Press Holdings), was fired in December

1986 because the government apparently viewed the quality of the journalism as poor and the editorial policy as uncoordinated. Lee, as well as other government ministers, were said to have been personally displeased with Lim.[9]

For years, government officials have toyed with the idea of bringing a team of government officers to the newspapers to ensure that the press becomes an effective spokesman for government policies. Lee considered sending top local scholars to the Graduate School of Journalism at Columbia University and then placing them in senior posts on local newspapers. Patrick Daniel, former aide to Lee Hsien Loon, the prime minister's son, has been a senior reporter on the *Straits Times* and has handled stories concerning the younger Lee, who is Minister of Trade and Industry. The absence of journalism courses at the National University of Singapore until quite recently is said to reflect the elder Lee's suspicions and low regard for journalism and journalists.

Radio and television, since 1980, have been run by the Singapore Broadcasting Corporation (SBC), a semigovernmental statutory board subsidized by the government and responsive to pressures of Lee's PAP. SBC Radio broadcasts mainly on four channels, each in one of the four official languages (English, Mandarin, Malay, and Tamil) for a total of 504 hours a week. A fifth channel, an FM stereo service, broadcasts 56 hours a week in English and Mandarin. Licenses are required for radio sets, and while many radios are unlicensed, radio listening has clearly increased, going from 114 sets per 1,000 people in 1970 to 182 sets per 1,000 in 1979. The number of radio licenses jumped from 236,856 in 1970 to 430,604 in 1979 and then to 607,843 in 1986.[10]

Television, as well, reaches practically every home in Singapore, with 498,730 licenses issued for a population of 2.6 million. Broadcasting is seen by the government as a powerful way of communicating not only information but also its social policies and cultural values. For example, SBC stopped transmitting serials in Cantonese and started dubbing them into Mandarin to back up formal education in Lee's "Speak Mandarin" campaign, which discouraged the use of diverse Chinese dialects.

SBC telecasts on the average of 140 hours per week on three channels. About 40 percent of these programs are produced by SBC itself, which is high indeed for a small country. These include dramas in Chinese, Malay, and Tamil and musical variety, educational, cultural, sports, and children's programs. In addition, imported dramas and documentaries are dubbed into Mandarin, Malay, and Tamil. But 55 percent of television programming is in English—a common language for many Chinese, Malay, and Indian people. Imported U.S. shows sometimes attract an audience of 300,000 to 400,000 people, but audiences for a locally produced drama in Chinese will attract as many as 800,000.[11] Locally produced Chinese dramas are sold abroad to China, Hong Kong, and Taiwan.

In addition, SBC Text, an electronic information service similar to the BBC's CEEFAX, provides free up-to-the-minute news and information to viewers from 6:00 A.M. to 12:00 P.M. (midnight) over two channels. The service reaches 70,000 households and requires a decoder to use.

SBC imports some excellent BBC television programs and broadcasts as well the BBC World Service on local VHF radio, receiving it by satellite from London.

SBC is a highly professional and admirable broadcasting service, but it is also clearly a government service, reflecting the views and policies of Lee Kuan Yew. During the contentious and sometimes violent years of 1959 to 1965, Lee and the PAP made effective use of broadcasting as a political weapon in their struggles against Communist groups.[12] With that background, not surprisingly, Lee and PAP today retain a firm control over broadcasting in Singapore.[13]

One factor that potentially threatens this government broadcasting monopoly has been the extraordinary increase in videocassette recorders, which by 1987 reached three out of four homes in Singapore—the highest average in Asia, higher than even Tokyo and Sydney.[14] Studies have shown that VCRs proliferate in countries, such as Saudi Arabia, where people can afford them and where television fare is dull, government controlled, and limited in choice of channels.

The popularity of VCRs may mean that Singaporeans will no longer be some of the world's most avid moviegoers. In 1979, there were 74 cinemas in Singapore with a seating capacity of 69,000, or about 29 seats per 1,000 people. This was an impressive increase from the 1970 total of 27,980 seats with only 14 seats per 1,000 people. By the 1980s, total annual attendance at cinemas was 46,054,000, with every Singaporean attending an average of 19.5 films per year.[15]

The spectacular growth of both media facilities *and* media participation during the 1970s and 1980s was accomplished against the backdrop of official suspicion, intolerance of criticism, and interference in public communication. Recently, Lee Kuan Yew has turned his attention to other, less pliable elements threatening his authority—foreign publications.

TAMING THE FOREIGN PRESS

The rising importance of the newly industrializing countries (NICs) of the Pacific Rim in the world economy has meant that Western news media are paying closer attention to business and political developments in Singapore, Malaysia, Hong Kong, Japan, Thailand, Taiwan, and South Korea. And with increasing frequency, those Asian governments frown on news reports that they feel tarnish their national image and perhaps make them less attractive to foreign investors. Western publications, including *Time, Newsweek,* the *Financial Times,* and the *Economist,* which carry periodic stories from roving correspondents, have had run-ins with regional Asian governments. But two highly professional publications, the *Asian Wall Street Journal,* a daily, and the *Far Eastern Economic Review,* a weekly, have had the most difficulty, especially in Singapore. Why? Because each publication maintains in each major Asian nation a full-time resident correspondent who reports regularly and in depth about local business and politics. Further, the *Journal* and the *Review* are widely read by business and political elites in each country. A series of incidents in recent years indicates that Lee Kuan Yew, who has the local Singapore media completely under his control, has decided to neutralize the foreign press as well. These press restrictions paralleled current government repression of political dissent and opposition.[16]

Lee's quarrels with foreign publications flared up in late 1986, beginning with *Time.* Under a newly passed press law, a 1986 amendment to the Newspaper and Printing Presses Act, the Minister of Communication was empowered to cut the Singapore circulation of any foreign publication for "engaging in domestic politics." *Time* had its circulation cut in half immediately, from 18,000 to 9,000 and later to 2,000 because of an article about government efforts to silence political opposition, in particular the treatment of one of only two opposition members of parliament. *Time* had refused to print in full a letter of complaint from Lee's press secretary. *Time* subsequently printed the letter in full, and sometime later the ban was lifted.

The *Asian Wall Street Journal* fell victim to the same law in February 1987 when Singapore effectively banned the *Journal* indefinitely because it too refused to publish a letter from a government official. For this, the government restricted the paper's local circulation of 5,000 to 400 copies daily. The story in question was not about "domestic politics" but a business story about a second securities exchange being established in Singapore. A government official wrote the *Journal* claiming the article contained errors of fact and that the reporter, Steven Duthie, was biased and prejudiced. The *Journal* responded that a meticulous investigation showed the article was accurate and that the paper would not publish a letter gratuitously charging a staff member with unprofessional conduct and alleging factual errors that did not exist. The *Journal*, however, did publish many letters concerning the controversy. The *Journal* invited the official to write another letter without the unfounded accusations, but he refused to do so. The circulation reduction soon followed.

This writer was in Singapore at the time and was fascinated by the government's response to criticisms of its action from various news organizations abroad. For a full two weeks, the lead story with a banner headline *every day* in the *Straits Times*, the leading English daily, and the major news item *every evening* on television news publicized the government's near-hysterical self-justification for its action against the *Journal*. If any proof were needed, this propaganda barrage certainly demonstrated how completely Lee controlled the local media and also that Lee was more concerned with local opinion than with views from overseas. Duthie and the *Journal* editors were surprised at the vehemence and length of the attacks on the *Journal* since Lee seemed determined to refute and discredit every response from abroad. Government supporters viewed such a response as evidence of Lee's toughness and ability to stand up to foreign pressures.[17]

Two months later, in April 1987, the *Far Eastern Economic Review*, a highly regarded regional journal which has been publishing in Hong Kong for over 40 years, was the next to feel the wrath of Lee Kuan Yew when renewal of the work permit of Nigel Holloway, its Singapore staffer, was denied. No explanation was given for what amounted to an expulsion, and the government withheld granting a visa to his successor. Some Singapore watchers felt the reason for the expulsion was that Holloway had a bylined story about Singapore in almost every issue of the *Review*. (In 1983, another *Review* staffer in Singapore, Patrick Smith, lost his work permit because of an alleged factual error in a story.) The *Review* later ended all circulation in Singapore.

Then, in December 1987, the ax fell again when Lee limited the *Review*'s weekly circulation to 500 copies, from the 10,000 regularly sold. Again, the stated reason was for involvement "in domestic politics" and that it had "consistently published distorted arti-

cles on Singapore." The dispute concerned a *Review* story about the
arrest of 22 alleged Marxists in May and June of 1987 that differed
from the official government version.

A third Hong Kong–based publication, *Asiaweek,* had its Singapore circulation slashed from 9,000 to 500 in October 1987, again
for "engaging in domestic politics in Singapore." This time, the government objected to the newsweekly's editing of a letter from a government official concerning the arrests of the same 22 accused
Marxists. In October 1988, Singapore partially removed the restric-
tion by raising *Asiaweek*'s permitted circulation to 5,000 copies.
This action followed the transfer of *Asiaweek*'s correspondent from
Singapore to Hong Kong. The correspondent, Lisa Beyer, claimed
her transfer was a concession to the government, but the magazine
denied it.[18]

Singapore's actions of sharply restricting, but not completely
banning, local distribution of these three papers is certainly a subtle
and effective form of censorship that from overseas does not appear
all that repressive. After all, no foreign journalist was jailed and
tortured and no newspapers closed down. But a definite "chilling
effect" was achieved: other foreign publications such as *Newsweek,
Time,* and the *International Herald Tribune* have shied away from
Singapore in their Asian reportage, and apparently that is the way
Lee Kuan Yew wants it.

Suppression of news about Singapore was certainly consistent
with Lee's longtime rejection of not only political opposition but
even forthright public discussion of economic and political affairs.
But what price was Singapore paying for its press restrictions?
First, relations with its trading partners, particularly the United
States, Britain, and Australia (who all support free press values),
became strained and somewhat sensitive.

Second, Singapore's hopes of becoming a regional media center,
as well as the major printing and publishing center of Southeast
Asia, were in jeopardy. In the past, some 82 foreign correspondents
were based in Singapore, but many have or plan to move away,
usually to Bangkok.[19] The *Asian Wall Street Journal, Far Eastern
Economic Review, International Herald Tribune,* the *Economist,
U.S.A. Today,* and other publications have been printed in part in
Singapore, but the trend is to find other printers in less oppressive
societies. In March 1988, the *Review* said it would cease printing
and publishing from Singapore, where it has been spending $1.48
million annually. Printing and publishing in Singapore grossed U.S.
$327 million in 1982 and employed 13,000 people; the recent

actions may have threatened future growth.[20]

Third, although some Singaporeans take a certain chauvinistic satisfaction in watching Lee stand up to the foreigners, there is no question that a good many Singaporeans, sophisticated and educated, are frustrated by the "soft authoritarianism" they live under. There is increased talk of a brain drain as younger Singaporeans seek opportunities in more open societies abroad. Finally, there is a good deal less news about Singapore in the world's press these days. And as one journalist said, "About 80 percent of the news that Western media report about Singapore is complimentary. But Lee doesn't want that negative 20 percent written either. He has scorn and contempt for the press and interferes with it as he does every other aspect of Singapore's public life."[21]

By 1991, there were indications that the press controversies were nearing resolution, with each side taking conciliatory steps toward settling the legal battles.

THE LESSONS OF LEE'S TIGHT LITTLE ISLAND

There are few places in the world where both a nation's major successes and shortcomings can be directly attributed to one man. But such is the case of Singapore and Lee Kuan Yew. Even his toughest critics, and he has many, credit Lee's policies for the extraordinary economic success of Singapore, and today, many feel that the current oppressive atmosphere will ease once Lee steps aside.

Having a brilliant leader is only one of the special circumstances of Singapore. As a small city-state, communication and economic interaction are easily accomplished. Unlike many Asian nations, Singapore is not burdened with millions of poor peasants living in remote areas. (This is not to say that Singapore is without its poor, most of whom are Malays.) Further, Singapore has not had a problem of rampant population increase. (In fact, Singapore is now encouraging its better educated married women to have more children.) Much credit must go as well to the hardworking and highly capable overseas Chinese, who are also central to the thriving economies of Taiwan and Hong Kong, as well as Malaysia and, to a lesser extent, Thailand and Indonesia.

Singapore's success seems related as well to its ties to Britain, its geographic location at the Straits of Malacca, its long traditions

of trading for survival, and, not least, the role of the English language, a window to the world and to international communication.
Even allowing for these special circumstances, Lee Kuan Yew's
Singapore still provides a fascinating case study in mass communication and development.

In Singapore, the media of mass communication and their audiences have clearly grown and expanded along with general economic development, and most of this has been accomplished in the
last 25 years. Media expansion has followed broad societal development, and possibly it accelerated development at later stages.

Again, the media and their audiences have floated upward on
the rising tide of economic growth. As individuals became better
educated and more literate, acquired both disposable income and
more leisure time, they made greater use of newspapers, radio, television, movies, and, more recently, VCRs. And as their audiences
increased and purchased the media-advertised products, so the media themselves prospered.

And although Lee's and now Goh's one-party government has
been paternalistic and authoritarian, it has also been efficient, competent, stable, and generally free of corruption. Such conditions
have often been lacking in African developing nations where ineffective and corrupt governments have thwarted media development.

Singapore has shown that if the economic and social opportunities for media development are present, then an authoritarian political atmosphere does not preclude media growth. However, a direct
result of Lee's "Singapore, Inc." is the lack of diversity: Singapore
Broadcasting Corporation controls *all* broadcasting and Singapore
Press Holdings owns and controls *all* of the major newspapers. (The
contrast with laissez-faire Hong Kong, with its over 50 diverse daily
newspapers and competing television and radio broadcasters, is
striking.)

For Singapore has shown that impressive mass communication
growth, as well as general economic expansion, can occur outside
the context of a democratic, participatory political system. This
seems to fly in the face of liberal political theory, which argues that
economic growth goes hand in hand with political freedom and
open societies.[22]

Singapore has adopted the rhetoric and precepts of capitalism:
investment, free trade, productivity, consumer markets, supply and
demand, and close ties to other Western economies. But Lee's government has shown little concern for press freedom, free flow of

information, and political pluralism. Singapore, Lee argues frequently, is a special situation that cannot afford the luxury of free expression.[23]

Nonetheless, economic and media development do generate strong desires for more democracy and human rights. Striving for these rights and better living conditions seems to be the strongest revolutionary force in the world today, as recent events in South Korea, the Philippines, Burma, Eastern Europe, and Chile have shown. To deal with this pressing challenge, strong "corporate states" such as Singapore, South Korea, and Taiwan will have to come up with creative ideas to deal with these political pressures which threaten to undo their impressive economic gains.

8

HONG KONG: TWILIGHT OF FREEDOM
WITHOUT DEMOCRACY

At first glance, Hong Kong appears to be much like Singapore. Both are small offshore city-states that have modernized rapidly by competing effectively in world trade, and both have been largely populated and driven by the diligent overseas Chinese.

But Hong Kong is still a British Crown Colony and will remain so until 1997 when it will return to Chinese control; the People's Republic of China has promised to make it a "special autonomous region," allowing it to continue its capitalist ways for 50 years. Under British rule, Hong Kong residents have had no vote; political decisions have long been made by colonial officials. No Lee Kuan Yew imposes his will; British rule has been largely benign and mostly hands off. "Freedom without democracy" is the term often applied.

For in the economic or business realm, Hong Kong entrepreneurs have enjoyed great freedom to make (or lose) money, and the prospect of making money has been a powerful engine driving that economic miracle. Mass communication in Hong Kong has successfully ridden on the back of that economic tiger and, unlike Singapore, enjoys the greatest freedom of any media system in Asia, outside of Japan.

This remaining remnant of empire had 5,800,000 people in 1991 compared with the 1976 population of 4,351,000. Over 97 percent were ethnic Chinese, many of whom had come as impoverished refugees from South China since 1948. Not until 1981 did the census record a majority actually born in Hong Kong. Only about 250,000 residents are Caucasians, mostly British, Americans, and Australians involved in business.

Hong Kong's millions are crowded onto 1,070 square kilometers (twice the size of Singapore), making it one of the most densely populated places on earth. Density per square kilometer was 5,192 in 1986. For the metropolitan areas of Hong Kong island—Kowloon, New Kowloon, and Tseun Wan—20,811 people occupy each square kilometer.

Hong Kong has been a spectacular economic success and is the third most important financial center in the world, after New York and London. With over 65,000 factories, Hong Kong has become a major global manufacturer; its economy is almost totally dependent on foreign trade. Hong Kong today is the world's leading exporter of textiles, toys, and watches. There are more Rolls Royces per capita than in any nation on earth.

What is the explanation for this spectacular economic and media development? The answer seems to lie in Hong Kong's history of unusual economic freedom. The island has progressed sharply since the 1940s when it was still very poor. Economist Peter Bauer believes that Hong Kong's success story is due to the aptitudes of the people and the pursuit of appropriate policies. "Enterprise, hard work, ability to spot and utilize economic opportunities are widespread in a population 97 percent Chinese engaged in the single minded pursuit of making money day and night," Bauer wrote.[1] Hong Kong seemed to break all the rules for economic development by stressing free trade, liberal immigration policies, low taxation, and minimal government involvement in commercial life. But more important, perhaps, there are no tax or other concessions to foreign investment and equally no restrictions on the withdrawal of capital or on the remission of profits. These liberal policies were intended to encourage foreign investment, which indeed they did.[2]

Hong Kong has had no foreign aid but was greatly aided by the influx of Shanghai business entrepreneurs who moved in, often with their factories, after the Chinese Communists took over the mainland in 1949. The colony at first provided scant social services, schooling, or literacy training for the flood of impoverished refugees. Nevertheless, the economy and the people flourished. But after the crisis of 1967, when the economy was brought to a standstill by riots related to the Cultural Revolution on the mainland, British authorities initiated a program to improve the quality of life by providing schools, housing, public transportation (including an exemplary subway and railroad system), social welfare programs, and roads.

All that has happened to the expanding economy has directly affected mass communication, of course, showing again that mass media seem to thrive in an open and free market economy. Hong Kong's media are truly *sui generis* for the non-Western world. In the numbers and variety of daily newspapers and other publications, the readership of Chinese papers, and the variety and sophistication of other media, especially television and motion pictures, Hong Kong is exceptional in Asia. Hong Kong makes more feature films annually than Hollywood.

Even more important, Hong Kong has unfettered freedom of media expression. Further, except for a few small Chinese communities in Western nations, Hong Kong is the only place where Chinese language newspapers enjoy freedom of the press. Publications banned in China, Taiwan, and Singapore are freely circulated in Hong Kong.

Some 560 publications were registered in 1986. Of these, 65 were newspapers: 51 Chinese language dailies; 2 English language dailies, *South China Morning Post* and *Hong Kong Standard;* 9 other English weeklies; 2 Japanese weeklies; and 1 bilingual paper. The 495 other periodicals included 322 in Chinese, 126 in English, 46 bilingual, and 1 trilingual.

This impressive array of publications is supported and supplemented by a printing and publishing industry of 3,370 printing factories, employing more than 32,000 people, plus more than 200 publishing houses, including some prominent book publishers from overseas.

Over the years, this free marketplace has tolerated the clash of ideas and news from diverse commercially oriented publications, as well as papers strongly supporting either the People's Republic of China or the Kuomintang regime on Taiwan.

In a country where 95 percent of the homes have television sets, television and radio play an important role in public communication and influence news coverage in the Chinese language newspapers. Hong Kong has two commercial television stations: Television Broadcasts (TVB) and Asia Television (ATV). Both have separate English and Chinese channels, so that four channels, reaching 5.1 million viewers, broadcast a daily average of 70 hours, or 17.5 hours for each channel. TVB, which began in 1967, has become the premier broadcaster in Hong Kong, with 80 percent of the viewers, compared to ATV's 20 percent. Both have young and energetic news teams, and each broadcasts about 14 hours a week of news shows on their English and Chinese channels. Both use a good deal of syndicated international news such as Visnews and WTN; in fact, both of their English news operations, in their format and style, sound a good deal like American television news programs.[3] English language television seems aimed at the 250,000 Americans, British, and Australians in residence, although the stations say that 80 percent of their audience are the bilingual Chinese. A good number of British soccer contests, as well as many popular U.S. television programs and movies, are regularly broadcast.

The British government owns and operates Radio Television Hong Kong (RTHK), which has its own radio station and transmits 14 hours of television programs weekly on the commercial channels. RTHK runs eight radio stations, three AM and five FM, and is considered to be fairly independent on news coverage. In fact, amid Hong Kong's climate of growing self-censorship, the state-owned RTHK has become one of the most independent-minded news outlets in Hong Kong. RTHK sounds a lot like the BBC (and relays a number of BBC shows) and carries much less of the "protocol news" which is a regular feature of government-controlled broadcasting in India and Singapore. (After 1997, RTHK is expected to become a part of the People's Republic propaganda network.)

The major radio outlet is the highly profitable Commercial Radio, which broadcasts 19 hours daily in English on an AM station and 24 hours daily in Chinese on both AM and FM channels. Commercial Radio's news and music, interspersed with advertisements, are widely listened to, not only in the Crown Colony but throughout South China. Commercial Radio broadcasts news every half hour: bulletins on the hour and headlines at the half hour. In addition, there are four major newsmagazine shows daily.[4]

Hong Kong's economic and political openness, plus its strategic location as a listening post and gateway to China, has long made it the major regional venue for foreign correspondents and international publications. Here can be found the main editorial offices of the *Far Eastern Economic Review,* the *Asian Wall Street Journal, Asiaweek, Asia* magazine, and the Chinese edition of *Reader's Digest.* In addition, 120 foreign correspondents for a wide range of world media—including *Time, Newsweek, International Herald Tribune,* and the *New York Times,* among others—work out of Hong Kong.

Hong Kong's laissez-faire economy and the opportunities to buy and sell media have attracted prominent publishers and entrepreneurs of the Western media world. Rupert Murdoch has owned the *South China Morning Post* since 1986; the Dow Jones Company has been there since launching its *Asian Wall Street Journal* and recently acquired full ownership of the *Far Eastern Economic Review*, an influential business and political journal in Asia. Allen Bond, a major business figure in Australia, purchased a big share of TVB from Sir Run Run Shaw, a legendary figure in Hong Kong's motion picture industry.

The media as well as their owners reflect the ethos of Hong Kong: hard-driving, risk-taking, and profit-seeking. As one editor said, "Money drives the place." The career of Sir Run Run Shaw, who has made many millions in producing and distributing motion pictures in Hong Kong and throughout the region, reflects this.

As in Singapore, the media have floated upward on the rising tide of economic development and individual prosperity. As people became more affluent, they purchased television sets, hi-fi equipment and VCRs, and attended more movies; for an increasing number of the industrious Chinese, there has been more leisure time in recent years to use the media.

The newspaper press, both in English and Chinese, typifies much of what is unique about Hong Kong, but it is not without its critics. A diplomat told us, "There is much self censorship, especially about relations with China. The press is tethered, not adversarial, and does little probing or investigative reporting. The press feels vulnerable about 1997 (when the PRC takes over) and keeps a certain distance; it is respectful of government."[5] To this observer, the two English dailies are informative, especially on foreign news, and professionally put together but somewhat cautious in reporting local government news. Another critic said the Chinese language press "feeds the average reader in Hong Kong with heavy doses of sex and violence, fashion and gossip, and sports and entertainment, but precious little weighty news and analysis."[6] Self-censorship by an economically free press is not equivalent to a government-controlled press, but it does indicate a press that fails to serve the political system by not providing incisive reports and comments on public affairs.

The most influential paper, the *South China Morning Post*, has, since its founding in 1903, been the voice of the economic powers that control Hong Kong and has always been close to the colonial authorities. (Interestingly, the word *colonial* is rarely heard in Hong Kong.) So there was much concern when, in November 1986, Rupert Murdoch bought control of the paper. Its 80,000 circulation is well ahead of its only English daily competition, the *Hong Kong Standard,* with 44,000 circulation. But the *Post*'s advertisements, rather than its news pages, are what makes it one of the most profitable newspapers of its size in the world. On one not particularly unusual Sunday in March 1988, the paper carried 122 pages of classified advertising. Profits for 1988 were projected at U.S. $48.8 million.[7] The paper covers news of New York, London, Beijing, and Tokyo, as well as sports results from throughout the English-speaking world. However, local critics feel that the Australian editors neglect local news and are somewhat obsequious to the Chinese while still being respectful of the British rulers.

The second-place *Hong Kong Standard* offers little competition, although some feel it covers Hong Kong better. The paper is a part of the Sing Tao group of companies headed by Sally Aw. In 1985, the company moved its corporate headquarters to Australia—reflecting its pessimism about 1997.

The Chinese language press has always been volatile, with papers frequently appearing and disappearing. In addition to a few large dailies, a swarm of "mosquito" papers devoted to special interests such as horse racing, crime, movies, and scandal flit in and out of the media scene.

The Hong Kong press has historically been divided into three ideological groupings: pro–Chinese Communist, pro-Kuomintang or Taiwan, and outright commercial undertakings such as the *Post.* In the last several decades, the pro-Communists and pro-Kuomintangs continued their feuding through newspaper columns, making Hong Kong a battleground of ideas and ideologies. Over the years, the Chinese papers became noted for reporting events in China and almost completely ignoring public affairs and developments within Hong Kong itself.[8] Recently, however, the Chinese press has become more concerned with local issues and has evolved, in effect, into a quasi-opposition to the British rulers.[9] The most recent concern is whether the press, both English and Chinese, will be able to continue to play a role in Hong Kong public life after 1997.

The major players have included the following:

Oriental Daily News, with 500,000 to 600,000 circulation, is the largest selling Chinese paper. It began as a "mosquito sheet" specializing in gambling and drug trafficking news, but after acquiring more skillful reporters, now specializes in sensational coverage of sex and violence and is read mainly by unskilled workers, housewives, and students.[10] Its owner runs the paper from Taiwan.

Sing Tao Jih Pao is owned by the Sing Tao group (Sally Aw), with about 70,000–120,000 circulation. The paper was started in 1939 to promote the KMT in wartime and has been a consistent money-maker.

Ming Pao recently became a major pro-Beijing paper and is owned by Louis Cha, a well-known kung fu novelist and supporter of Deng Xiaoping's economic policies. With 115,000 circulation, the paper has thrown in its lot with the coming merger of Hong Kong with China and believes the future holds promise.

The five pro-Communist papers—*Ta Kung Pao, New Evening Post, Wen Wei Po, Ching Po,* and *Hong Kong Commercial Daily*— have a combined readership of only 255,000, or 5 percent of the major newspapers' readership. However, as the transition nears, more people read these papers for information on the future.

Sing Pao Daily News, owned by Ho Man Fat, is politically middle to left. Pro-KMT in the late 1970s, it is now moving toward the People's Republic as 1997 nears. With over 200,000 circulation, the paper stresses crime news that is very popular with Chinese readers. Miranda Yui, a former journalist, says the paper reports what the government wants publicized but rarely criticizes it and practices much self-censorship.[11] (The same criticism can be made of most papers.) Major problems facing the Chinese press, she said, were inexperienced and untrained reporters, low standards for news coverage, and concern that the papers will increasingly tilt toward the PRC, thus sacrificing the diversity the press now enjoys.

But why so many papers in Hong Kong? The papers are inexpensive to produce since most run only 12, 16, or 20 pages at most; many people read two or three papers; and finally, with so many entrepreneurs with money around and no government interference, starting up a newspaper is easily accomplished.

Emily Lau, an astute observer of the Hong Kong press, believes that in the absence of democratic institutions, the news media could play an important part in public life in Hong Kong. "But, the news media do not seem equipped to do this, nor do they appear to be in the mood to take up the challenge," she wrote. "Instead, many are already leaning over backward to please Beijing. Some do it because it is good for business; others think that Chinese dominance is inevitable and that it is futile to try to resist it. . . . Like the businessmen, they want a few more stable and prosperous years to make money before they pull out."[12] But others argue that the press is free and reasonably responsible even though it practices self-censorship toward news relating to China.

MEDIA RELATIONS WITH THE BRITISH

The media have obviously prospered under the colonial rulers, and journalists are aware of the freedom they enjoy. Nonetheless, relationships between the British officials, Chinese journalists, and media moguls have long been ambiguous and sometimes abrasive. By and large, the British have kept their hands off the press even though they have their own broadcast system (RTHK) and maintain an efficient Government Information Service (GIS), which supplies the media with all kinds of information and subtly influences public opinion.

The British have had some rather draconian laws on their books but have rarely invoked them. The press has had little legal freedom due to this myriad of legal controls, but the British have refrained from imposing them and the docile press has not tested the laws.

But in March 1987, the colonial government contributed greatly to the press's growing anxiety by enacting the Public Order (Amendment) Bill, making it an offense for any person to publish "false news likely to cause alarm to the public . . . or disturb public order." Anyone found guilty is liable to a fine of HK$100,000 and a mandatory two years of imprisonment. This action set off a great uproar among journalists and civil libertarians. With uncharacteristic unity, the local and foreign press denounced "the high handedness" of the British, and one Chinese paper said that freedom of the press was dead. Some thought the usually docile Chinese papers had overreacted, but it did reflect real concerns about their future.

Few worried about the British applying the law, but many feared the law will be used by the PRC to control the press after 1997. This episode was preceded several months earlier by a well-intentioned effort by the British attorney general to repeal several archaic and largely forgotten press laws (which gave government the right to close down newspapers and presses). But it was decided to retain the "false news" portions to enable the government to deal with a possible riot situation.

Many in Hong Kong did not see it that way and accused the British of undermining efforts of local residents to increase democratic safeguards before the PRC takes over. Barry Wain, managing editor of the *Asian Wall Street Journal,* said, "In the absence of any reasonable explanation of the press law, I can only conclude that the British are doing this because they think it will please China."[13]

Many people of Hong Kong have been calling for free, direct elections, reasoning that if the colony is self-governed before 1997, their bargaining position with the PRC will be stronger. Beijing, however, opposes the elections, and the British authorities and some newspapers have been reluctant to push for these elections for fear of offending the Beijing government.

Nonetheless, the landmark direct elections did take place in September 1991, sending a clear message to China and Britain that Hong Kong residents want greater democracy. In the first direct legislative elections ever held there, the liberal pro-democracy faction won 16 of 18 seats contested. Not one pro-China candidate won despite a barrage of warnings from pro-China newspapers. Little real political power was at stake but the election was considered a real gauge of public sentiment.

The episode illustrates the ideological shifts occurring in Hong Kong. Twenty years ago, the Chinese Communists, who tried to import the Cultural Revolution into Hong Kong, were considered the radicals, but today they are the conservatives. Today's radicals are the journalists such as Emily Lau and many others calling for free elections and self-rule in the colony.

The residents' concerns about what many see as a British sell-out were heightened even more when it was revealed in March 1987 that colonial authorities had been censoring films in Hong Kong for 34 years without legal authority. And the main reason for censoring some films and banning others was the British concern about not offending the People's Republic of China.[14]

XINHUA: THE SHADOW GOVERNMENT

In recent years, Xinhua, or the New China News Agency, has become the shadow government of Hong Kong and is becoming increasingly powerful politically as the 1997 transition date nears. The agency's Hong Kong Bureau employs more than 600 persons and until recently maintained the facade of only being a news agency instead of a government-in-waiting. Within the Xinhua bureau is a counterpart for every British colonial official, and the Beijing presence is being increasingly felt, especially in the press.

A U.S. editor noted that the day is past when actions of the British governor are big news. "When the Governor returned to London for consultations, it was hardly mentioned. When shortly afterward, the head of Xinhua left suddenly for Beijing during some riots there, the Hong Kong stock market took a tumble."[15]

Some observers think the Xinhua presence contributes directly to self-censorship by the press and the timidity shown by film-makers. "There is a sense of confusion in the media. Most think it best to keep your head down and don't make trouble because someone may be taking names, and they may be," said Patrick Smith of the *International Herald Tribune*.[16] The press, he said, reflects a growing pessimism about future relations with China. With it has come a concern about the British, who the press feels are not standing up to Beijing; there are concerns the British are already forsaking Hong Kong and making handshake deals with Beijing to protect their own interests, Smith said.

PRC representatives are certainly trying to co-opt the Chinese press by offering trips to Beijing, free dinners, gifts, and other enticements to Hong Kong journalists. "It's easy to co-opt the Chinese press; they're young, underpaid, untrained, and easily bought due to lack of ethics and standards. So it's not surprising."[17]

Many Hong Kong journalists have either softened their critical stance toward China or defected to the Communist camp journalistically. A dwindling number of Hong Kong journalists are willing to risk antagonizing Beijing, and some have even quit their profession because they fear future restrictions. "Many newspapers here are voluntarily giving up their freedom of speech without a fight. Come 1997, imagine what will happen. It's a pity," said Lin Xi Ling, a visiting scholar and a dissident who left China for France in 1984.[18]

The press has been accused of not reporting the increasing exodus of Hong Kong residents to other nations. It has been estimated that about 3 to 5 percent are leaving annually; these, not surprisingly, are mostly young professionals—the more affluent business people important to the economy. In 1991, it was expected that another 500,000 people would emigrate by 1997. But most ordinary people are predicted to stay.

By 1993, the future of Hong Kong is expected to become about 90 percent clear, and the atmosphere for press freedom is expected to plummet further. By that time, some of the foreign publications based in Hong Kong such as the *Far Eastern Economic Review* and *Asian Wall Street Journal* may be making plans to leave, possibly to Bangkok or Japan. The *Journal* plans to stay in Asia, but a possible move out of Hong Kong does not create undue problems. Derek Davies, who has been editor of the *Review* since 1965, would be reluctant to move out of Hong Kong. "Hong Kong has been a superb watchtower in Asia but we are not sure we can stay after 1997."[19]

Hong Kong's hopes for continued prosperity and freedom after 1997 were dealt a severe blow on June 4, 1989, when Chinese troops opened fire on pro-democracy student demonstrators in Beijing. The students' call for a more open and democratic China had been widely supported by large demonstrations in Hong Kong, so there was much despair after the suppressions. Afterwards, the Chinese government refused to agree not to station troops in Hong Kong and also resisted efforts from Hong Kong to establish a bill of rights for Hong Kong citizens before the takeover. Then in January 1990, Beijing drafted a Basic Law that would limit to 18 the number of elected seats in Hong Kong's 60-member legislature, thus leaving the huge majority to be manipulated by China. As a result, a deepening sense of despair and betrayal has gripped Hong Kong.

CONCLUSIONS

The press and other media of Hong Kong have been much criticized recently, and for good reasons. On the other hand, there has been diversity and, at least for a while, real freedom. But as Albert Camus said, freedom is only a chance for the press to be better whereas enslavement is a certainty of the worst.

Have the Hong Kong media taken advantage of their opportunity to be a real Fourth Estate and play an important role in public opinion? No. However, the international media located there, especially the *Far Eastern Economic Review* and the *Asian Wall Street Journal*, have contributed greatly to local news coverage. (The *Journal*, for example, revealed the illegal film censorship by the British.)

The unparalleled freedom both to make money and to use mass communication for all kinds of purposes has made Hong Kong a *rara avis* in the world's media aviary. Although its days of freedom seem to be clearly numbered, Hong Kong does seem to have provided students of international communication with these lessons: If the media are free to operate in an open market economy such as Hong Kong, then the media and their audiences will certainly grow and prosper as the economic sector grows and prospers. And, if the role of government is to provide a stable and constitutional setting for that economic realm, and if the ruling government essentially leaves the media alone, as the British colonial rulers have done, then the media will do well.

Such, generally, have been the relations between the economy, the government, and the media of Hong Kong over the last several decades. Hong Kong has been a fascinating media show while it has lasted. But after the massacre of Tiananmen Square, the prospects were not promising.

By 1992 it was apparent that 1997 had already arrived. The People's Republic had moved into Hong Kong both economically and politically in a major way. Economists reported that Beijing was by then the biggest investor in Hong Kong, with most estimates exceeding $10 billion.[20] Whatever the final contours of the political economy are after 1997, it is very unlikely that Hong Kong's remarkable freedom of the press will last into the next century.

III

SUMMING UP

9

CHANGING THEORY AND IDEOLOGY

The Africanist geographer, George H. T. Kimble, once wrote that Africa is a bad place for the theorizers or generalizers because Africa had so often proved them wrong. Certainly as far as communication theory goes, this seems to be true in some respects during the first quarter century of self-rule in Africa (and perhaps in Asia). It may be useful, therefore, to consider the relevance of several strands of communication theory and political ideology to what has actually happened to mass communication in these African and Asian countries.

To this observer, it appears that much of what has been written over the past 30 years about the interactions of communication and development (or social change) bears faint relevance to the African experience or, for that matter, to India, Singapore, and Hong Kong. In addition, the political ideology that has accompanied many of the social engineering efforts in the new African states has contributed, I believe, both to Africa's general plight and to that of its press.

Two prominent economists expressed my view when criticizing their own field. Lester Thurow wrote, "To my mind what mainstream American economists do reflects more an academic need for an internal theoretical consistency and rigor than it reflects observable, measurable realities in the world we live in."[1] And Peter T. Bauer wrote that the central theme of his 1981 book "is the conspicuous and disconcerting hiatus (gap) between accepted opinion and evident reality in major areas of academic and public economic discourse since the Second World War."[2] To my mind, both Thurow and Bauer could have been talking about various mass communication and development studies.

Since the war, there have been changing patterns or fashions in media-related social research—fashions that have gone out of style, sometimes belatedly, as objective conditions in the world have changed. As Ithiel Pool wrote, "This is not abnormal; it is the way social sciences usually move. Most social research is motivated by social problems or social changes; researchers respond to real-world crises by coming up with ideas for research. If these turn out to be fruitful, they are mined over and over until the vein begins to run out. Then social changes stimulate a new surge of different research."[3]

Changing trends in communication research seem to reflect the great dramas in the international political economy and fall into several distinct time periods.

1. The period from the 1950s into the mid-1960s was the time of decolonization of the great European empires and the "emergence" of the Third World. This was the heyday of foreign aid and countless development projects as Western nations assisted the new nations on the road to modernization. The dominant paradigm, or principal research approach, was essentially the empirical social science approach, practiced mainly in America, that investigated the roles that mass and interpersonal communication played in the process of "nation building." The classic study (and the target of much subsequent criticism) was Daniel Lerner's *The Passing of Traditional Society* published in 1956.

This period extending into the 1970s also marked the high tide of Third World socialism in both Africa and Asia, as well as the emergence of the one-party state and the developmental concept of the press.

2. The 1970s were generally a period of disillusionment and acrimonious charges of blame. By then, many billions in foreign aid and grandiose development projects had failed to produce modern, viable new nations. It became the fashion to condemn the aid-giving Western nations for "underdeveloping" the new nations and for keeping them economically subservient to their former colonial masters. And the dominant paradigm was rancorously attacked by critics from Europe and Latin America, many of whom came from Marxist scholarly traditions; they blamed the Western nations and their media for Third World failures. Charges of "media imperialism" were directed against Western media, and calls came at UNESCO and other forums for a "new world information and commun-

ication order" to redress the imbalances and inequities in international communication.

3. The 1980s ushered in yet another dramatic swing in the world's political economy. A seminal trend was the widespread recognition of the failure of socialism as a viable economic system. Robert Heilbroner, the eminent economist, wrote:

> Less than seventy five years after it officially began, the contest between capitalism and socialism is over: capitalism has won. The Soviet Union, China, and Eastern Europe have given us the clearest possible proof that capitalism organizes the material affairs of mankind more satisfactorily than socialism: however inequitably or irresponsibly the marketplace may distribute goods, it does so better than the queues of a planned economy; however mindless the culture of commercialism, it is more attractive than state moralism; and however deceptive the ideology of a business civilization, it is more believable than that of a socialist one. [4]

While the capitalist Western nations and Japan surged ahead economically, the socialist nations could not point to even one successful economy. The former USSR, China, and Eastern Europe publicly rejected the centralized planning of socialism and sought economic reforms that looked surprisingly like free enterprise capitalism. Numerous African nations, such as Tanzania, Guinea, and Ghana, which had been modelled on socialist economies, had proved dismal failures. The dramatic economic successes of the "Four Tigers" of the Pacific Rim (South Korea, Singapore, Hong Kong, and Taiwan) were achieved without foreign aid but with market economies based on trade with the West. These Asian success stories also told us something as well about media development.

Many Third World nations, beset with overwhelming debts, sought to reorient their economies to the needs and opportunities of the new global economy. In March 1990, even the president of Ethiopia, Colonel Mengistu Haile Mariam, proposed scrapping Ethiopia's rigid Soviet-style economic system and replacing it with a mixed economy. Similar sentiments came out of Mozambique, another failed Communist state. (Independent India as well has moved from its socialist beginnings toward a market economy.) With the decline of socialism came the decline of the Communist and developmental models of mass communication. With the resurgence of capitalism came a newfound recognition of the values of a free and independent media system, one anchored in a market economy and removed from political controls.

This changed world of the 1990s provides an opportunity to look again at the growth of media systems from the perspective of recent history.

ONE-PARTY STATE AND DEVELOPMENTAL PRESS CONCEPT

The one-party system of government was adopted throughout Africa to offset the divisive tendencies exacerbated by ethnic and communal frictions as well as linguistic and religious differences. As Xan Smiley wrote:

> Indeed, there is a very good case for a single party system. Multi-party politics in Africa has invariably deteriorated into a competition between tribal blocs or alliances. In addition, the concept of a loyal opposition, presupposing some basic national consensus usually absent in Africa, is considered by most Africans to be crazy: neither that consensus nor any form of liberal individualist tradition exists. Peoples' attitudes are fiercely determined by ties of family and clan. At its gentlest, politics means that a opposition will be absorbed by traditional African palaver into the single party; if not, then it is silenced, perhaps violently. The secret ballot becomes unnecessary. . . . So rigid control—which easily slides into repression and authoritarianism—is the order of the day, and the leadership, lacking any stimulating competition from within, becomes fossilized. This process has occurred in almost every single-party state in Africa.[5]

The usual way to change such unresponsive governments has been the coup d'état; one-party states do not vote themselves out of office. Consequently, for much of black Africa, the choice has been single-party civilian rule or a military junta. Significantly, the basic single-party pattern was found both in radical African socialist states such as Nkrumah's Ghana and in Houphouet-Boigny's conservative, "neocolonialist" Ivory Coast, the most economically successful state in black Africa.

Despite what some enthusiastic political scientists wrote in the 1960s, the one-party state was not a new form of democracy. Even such leaders as Kenneth Kaunda of Zambia and Julius Nyerere of

Tanzania—men of laudable personal ideals whose development programs, Humanism and Umjaama respectively, were taken seriously
by the West—have destroyed all vigorous, constructive political discussion, because they feared it.[6] And with good reason, for had
there been parliamentary democracy in Zambia and Tanzania, both
leaders would have been voted out of office years ago by disillu-
sioned Africans. In 1992, Nyerere publicly admitted that mistakes
had been made and that Tanzania must build afresh. It was, and is,
rare indeed, anywhere in independent Africa, for the incumbents to
be voted out. Of the 41 countries in sub-Saharan Africa, only 5—
Botswana, Mauritius, Senegal, Gambia, and newly independent
Namibia—qualified technically as multi-party democracies.

Military rule has not proved much of an improvement either. In
most cases, the soldiers became a law unto themselves, and this
resulted in a breakdown of what legal order existed and a suspen-
sion of whatever constitution had been in place. One U.S. correspondent wrote:

> In much of Africa, the warrior caste has evolved into a ruling
> caste. Soldiers, policemen and militias have become members of
> a privileged elite, free to inflict their will or whim on the citi-
> zenry. They are fed and clothed while peasants starve and dress
> in rags. They are issued guns and bullets while farmers lack
> hoes and seeds. And in many countries, they are accountable to
> no one—not to politicians, not to the press, not to the public they
> are pledged to serve.[7]

Military rule has been characterized by a rejection of politics
because politicians and democracy were blamed for national failures, even in nations where there had been precious little democracy. Yet a successful military regime, whether in Africa or elsewhere, is difficult to find.

Military juntas usually were even more restrictive of free expression and diverse political discourse than one-party civilian
rulers. But there was some truth in the justification the soldiers
used when taking control: in the one-party governments, overem-
phasis was placed on politics and political solutions, to the neglect
of economic development, notably agriculture and traditional mar-
keting systems. Kwame Nkrumah had said, "Seek ye first the political kingdom" and all else would follow. By politicizing the economy
and launching expensive, inefficient, state-run enterprises, Nkrumah rapidly depleted Ghana's balance of payments surplus. By the
mid-1960s, the country had accumulated a mountain of foreign

debt and a low international credit rating, and Ghana has been mostly, as Africans say, "in the hands of the soldiers" ever since.

One-party rule, such as Nkrumah's regime, produced a neo-Communist model of communication for much of Africa.[8] This authoritarian pattern for African mass communication has been euphemistically called the "developmental concept" of the press.[9] This concept is congruent with the mobilization politics of the one-party state. "Harambee," as Kenyatta said, "let's all pull together." The theory also fit in well with a centralized, all-powerful government that would use the media to aid in the great tasks of nation building and political integration.

This developmental concept, as found in Africa, has much in common with Lee Kuan Yew's heavy-handed control of Singapore's media. But in contrast with much of anglophone Africa, development did occur in Singapore, much as it did in the Ivory Coast. Over the years, Lee justified his repressions of the press by resorting to the rationales of the developmental concept.

The basic weakness of the model was that it became just another manifestation of neo-Communist authoritarian rule, and the media—press, radio, television, news agencies, information services—all became a part of government itself. The basic function of the media, as in the Soviet Union (at least before Gorbachev), was to publicize government policies, to control the people, and to maintain the current regime in power.

The press, then, did not act as a check on government nor as a critic of official policies or actions. The press provided neither reliable information nor an informed discussion of public affairs. Politicians received no feedback on public opinion. As the new governments slid down the slippery slope of corruption, repression, and stagnation, African journalists were powerless to even report the situation, much less criticize it.

It became apparent that the centralized, government/party control of all public communication, the ineffective use of media as tools of development, and the suppression of competing voices or of even mild dissent (as happened so often) did not produce good newspapers or even many readers interested in what those papers had to say. The same was true of radio and television, where government control was even more complete.

By the 1980s, it was clear that the one-party state or its variant, the military junta, had not produced either newspapers or broadcasting services of a very high order. As a result, these government-controlled media contributed little to either public opinion or to national development. The developmental concept of the press, which was closely allied to the precepts of African socialism, has to a great extent become a rationalization or justification for authoritarian controls of a society. When one looks closely at what an official newspaper reports or does not report, one sees that political control, not development goals, are its raison d'être. Its main function, as with broadcasting, is to maintain unpopular oligarchies in power.

Singapore, as we saw, offers an interesting variation on this African model. Under Lee Kuan Yew and his People's Action Party, political control of the media and repression of political opposition were nearly complete, but in the economic realm, an efficient, trade-oriented economy operated effectively. Among the one-party states of Africa, only the Ivory Coast and Kenya, with their capitalist economies, managed to improve their peoples' standards of living. But political turmoil threatens hard-won economic gains in both nations.

DOMINANT PARADIGM OF COMMUNICATION RESEARCH

During the 1950s and 1960s, a number of American social scientists argued that communication—mass and interpersonal—had a distinct role to play in the national development of the newly emerging nations, as they were called. In simplified form, it was argued that "where there is communication, there is development and where there is development, there is communication." Most communications scholars agreed on this.

Some argued that a closer, almost causal, relationship existed in the process whereby media usage helped create modern "empathic" people and aided the development process.[10] This so-called dominant paradigm has been associated with the names of Daniel Lerner, Wilbur Schramm, Ithiel Pool, Lucian Pye, Fred Frey, and others. This approach was characterized by optimistic efforts at national development, fueled by great infusions of foreign aid, which marked the first years of political independence during the 1960s.

Later, as most of the new nations foundered, especially in Africa, and did *not* prosper, the dominant paradigm came in for a good deal of criticism by the critical and/or neo-Marxist scholars, who announced that it had been rejected or at least had had its day.

But has it? Perhaps just the conditions that produced the model and the "vein of research to be mined" had changed. The West's mammoth and idealistic efforts to aid the development of the Third World in the 1960s had produced few tangible results. The few successes of real development occurred in free market, trading states, such as Hong Kong, Singapore, Taiwan, and South Korea, where impressive development came without foreign aid and centralized planning. But, interestingly, critics of the dominant paradigm paid scant attention to these successful nations.

Loss of faith both in the effectiveness of foreign aid itself and in the ability of African governments to deal successfully with their own intractable problems led to widespread disillusionment with planned and controlled programs of social change and the expected role that communication would play in development and modernization.

Certain aspects of that model of communication and development certainly can be criticized as being too deterministic, too optimistic (and perhaps naive), too unilinear, and too generalized. In addition, it can be argued that too little concern is paid to local problems and barriers to development, and too much emphasis is placed on strong central governments and the idea of harnessing communication in many forms to aid development.

A major shortcoming of this research approach was that it tended to ignore or underestimate the impact of politics and political coercion on mass communication, particularly the press. Lerner had argued that as a nation developed, political participation gradually increased so that in time, a democratic polity would evolve. This liberal model of development failed to anticipate Lee Kuan Yew's Singapore or South Korea, where economic growth accompanied authoritarian rule.

Social theorists sometimes tended to ignore the real world of political repression when spinning their theories. Official repression of free expression was a central reason that free and independent newspapers atrophied in Africa, yet this factor was often glossed over by sympathetic social scientists, many of them doing contract research for the developing countries or involved in development projects. India's experiences since its independence offers a counterexample of how a free press managed to survive political pressures and thus assisted democracy to survive.

A related concern was the heavy-handed government control of the economies, wherein inefficient parastatal corporations and centralized planning replaced the traditional market economies of African societies. However, it is encouraging to note that in recent years, under the pressures of huge debts and International Monetary Fund prodding, many African nations have moved toward privatization and market economies.

Still, much of value can be found in the dominant paradigm. I believe this research tradition has been unfairly criticized by academic critics, who are much less rigorous in their own research and fail to base their conclusions on hard evidence, as have the scholars they criticized.

The basic underlying thesis that media systems grow with social systems and that communication is both an indicator of and a contributor to development still holds true. Development can contribute to communication, and communication in turn aids development, if the conditions are right. That basic proposition is still valid and has not been successfully refuted. Certainly Singapore and Hong Kong provide examples of societies where, in general, impressive media development has accompanied (or perhaps followed) impressive economic development. The recent growth of the Indian economy, which has been accompanied by a marked growth in both print and television markets, is further corroboration of this view.

On the other hand, the African experience reminds us that the barriers or obstacles to development can at times be so formidable that little economic development, in the Western sense, takes place, and what there is seems little affected by the rudimentary and inadequate communication media that are in place.

Africa's deep-seated problems—poverty, disease, hunger and malnutrition, ethnicity, linguistic diversity, ineffective governments, rudimentary economic systems—and their political and social consequences are so pervasive in so many countries that the meager media systems and national development efforts have foundered. Small wonder that mass communication does not seem to make much difference.

Moreover, Africa teaches us the persistence of traditionalism. Traditional ways of doing things continue to be barriers to communication and development; I believe these factors have been underrated and at times ignored. Modernization is coming to Africa, but mainly in a few urban areas and at a much slower pace than was generally expected. Beneath that veneer of Western education and dress of the bright, articulate African bureaucrat or newspaper editor is a traditional African with strong continuing ties to his extended family, his clan, his ethnic group, and his *weltanschauung.*

In matters of communication, Africans have long had informal ways of exchanging news and information, and these continue to be

used. Perhaps a major shortcoming of mass communication systems, including newspapers, is the failure to tie modern media onto
the traditional channels of communication and so to reach the villages where most Africans live. Perhaps that is why the daily newspaper is still a "European" or foreign institution that has yet to
become an intregal part of the social fabric of Africa.

CRITICAL APPROACHES

Fashions in communication research change with the times,
and when, by the late 1960s, it became apparent that independent
Africa was *not* developing as expected, several things happened in
the world of international communication theory.

First, as mentioned, the dominant paradigm, with its stress on
foreign aid and development projects, was widely criticized as a
neocolonialist conspiracy to help keep African and other new nations underdeveloped and dependent on their former colonial masters. But more important, the paradigm was rejected as being inappropriate and ineffective for the Third World in general.

Next, it was argued that if Africa was stagnant, it was due to
outside or external influences—the Western capitalist and/or former
colonial nations were keeping the continent in a condition of economic servitude and dependency. And if this were true, then the
Western media must be participating in this effort to keep down
Third World media and maintain Western dominance in communications as well. Hence, "media imperialism."

These approaches of European critical and neo-Marxist scholars
to explain international communication problems became more
fashionable in some academic circles as well as in international
bodies such as UNESCO. By the early 1970s these trends led to the
rising controversy over a "new world information order."

From the perspective of this writer, who has observed mass
communication in Africa for 25 years, it is difficult to imagine what
the press and broadcasting would be like in Africa today *without*
the pervasive Western influence described earlier. Without that European impact, both colonial and postcolonial, African media would
be severely diminished today.

Two of the weakest media systems in Africa today are found in
Liberia and Ethiopia, two nations which were never colonized.
Much of British colonialism proved deleterious for Africa, but the

influence of journalism seemed to be an exception. For the best of African journalism, meager though it still is, is essentially Western-oriented and a product of modern Western society. The best and most positive aspects of African journalism (as well as the worst) are rooted in practices borrowed from the West.

The free press of India, of course, is an admirable example of Western-influenced journalism contributing to the free press that has made possible over 40 years of Indian democracy. That African journalists and their media have not measured up to those of India is due to political and social conditions within Africa itself, not because of some foreign conspiracy.

And yet a whole school of academic critics have in recent years decried this whole process of Western communication influences as media imperialism and have seen this cultural incursion as a malevolent conspiracy to dominate the media of these former colonies. They have joined calls at UNESCO and elsewhere for a new world information order to right alleged communication wrongs inflicted on a passive and victimized Africa.[11] The hotly debated topic is slowly but clearly fading away. In May 1990, a United Nations committee dealing with information policy unanimously approved a resolution that bade farewell to the proposal.

In their mass media, as in much else, the new Africa was perceived as being "dependent" on Europe for its very existence, and for all it knows because of an insidious "one-way flow of information" from North to South. The Western news agencies—Associated Press, Reuters, Agence France Presse, and United Press International—were singled out for particular criticism.

However, in Africa, those nations which have maintained the closest ties to Europe, such as the Ivory Coast to France and Kenya to Britain, have been the most successful economically, most politically stable, and have had the most effective media systems. However, as the 1990s opened, both the Ivory Coast and Kenya were beset with internal turmoil, due largely to pressures for greater democratic freedoms and economic reforms. Africans who have received the greatest amount of "one-way flow" of information, knowledge, and cultural fare—through education abroad, books and news media from overseas, technology transfer, as well as movies and television programs—are the ones that have progressed and developed most. This is even more apparent in the economic successes of Singapore and Hong Kong, where Western media and mass culture have been so pervasive. Japan, of course, is the prime example of an Asian nation that successfully competed with the

West by adopting Western ways in economics, science, and technology.

Guinea, a West African nation that deliberately cut its ties from France at independence, is one of the saddest examples of economic stagnation and retrogression, in part because it chose to isolate itself from Western information flows and thus from participation in the modern world. The same can be said for Myanmar (formerly Burma), a former British colony that has deteriorated badly since its military socialist government closed its doors to the outside world in 1962.

The problem for some of the critics is that they try to impose on Africa and the Third World certain frameworks and predispositions that have been developed elsewhere, often in pristine academic corridors where collectivist and neo-Marxist ideas are still popular, although Marx's ideas have been increasingly rejected by the real world of politics and economics, including, of course, the former Soviet Union. (It is also true that the dominant paradigm of media development is a product of Western academics and was applied to Third World nations through various development projects.) Some critics argue that mass communication in Africa has been victimized by a conspiracy of multinational corporations. But anyone familiar with journalism in Africa can see that the few newspapers of value and usefulness to African readers are the very papers with European roots and traditions. Or such critics fail to perceive that educated Africans who try to keep up with the outside world and with Africa itself rely on "multinational media" such as the BBC World Service, *Le Monde*, Voice of America, *International Herald Tribune, Time, Newsweek*, the *Economist*, and *Financial Times* to supplement their own meager news media.

Many critical media researchers, as well as Africanist scholars, have evidenced a strong sympathy toward socialist approaches to national development, even after these efforts proved disastrous failures; to date, few of these scholars appear to have reevaluated these "false starts." In the 1960s, Western scholars lavishly praised the socialist experiments of Nkrumah in Ghana, Toure in Guinea, and Nyerere in Tanzania but pointedly ignored what Felix Houphouet-Boigny was doing in Abidjan to continue French economic involvement in the Ivorian economy or what Jomo Kenyatta was doing in Nairobi to hold onto British capital investment and expertise. Despite their development gains, compared with the rest of black Africa, the Ivory Coast and Kenya were besmirched with the odious term of "neocolonialism" and ignored by many scholars.

In the same way, the spectacular economic growth of the Four Tigers (Taiwan, Singapore, South Korea, and Hong Kong) were largely ignored during the 1970s.

Ideological blinders have prevented many communications scholars from seeing and acknowledging what has happened. They emulate and refine each other's arguments, but few have had first-hand experience of what happens to news media trying to develop under the harsh authoritarianism of one-party and military rule. As a result, their explanations seem far removed from the real world and are often ridiculed by journalists and others who are familiar with contemporary Africa.

NEW THINKING OF 1980s

Again, fashions in social theories are changing with the times. And the theories of hegemony, structuralism, and dependency seemed to be less in vogue in the 1990s. Now there is less blaming of Europe and the United States for "underdeveloping Africa" (as one book title had it) and more finger pointing, this often by the Africans themselves, at the African governments and their leaders.

A growing consensus has been developing that Africa's myriad problems have been largely of its own making, due in large part to bad government, corruption, and misguided policies. And under state control of media systems, Africans themselves learned little about their problems from their newspapers and broadcasting.

"African socialism" has proved a failure in Africa, with not a single success to point to. Whether it went by the name of Pan Africanism, Negritude, Humanism, Ujamaa, Mobutisme, or African Socialism, it hasn't worked. This is all part, of course, of a worldwide retreat during the 1980s from socialist economic methods.

Two of the most prosperous countries in Africa are still considered colonies by some, but their economies are capitalist. The Ivory Coast is officially independent, but its wealth is managed by 27,000 Frenchmen who have put the country's economy at the top of the African league, judged by every possible yardstick of productivity and development. As James Brooke reported,

> In a continent oppressed by famine, the Ivory Coast is black Africa's largest agricultural exporter. In a continent of economic decay, the Ivory Coast has raised its per capita income from $70 at independence to $610 today, second only to South Africa

among African nations that do not profit from exporting oil. Another measure of prosperity, per capita gross national product,
was $720 in the Ivory Coast in 1986; the average per capita GNP
for the rest of sub-Saharan Africa was $390. . . . In a continent
made unstable by coups, the Ivory Coast has been run by the
same civilian president, Felix Houphouet-Boigny, since independence.[12]

(But Houphouet, who at 84 was the oldest and longest-serving African leader, came under growing political opposition in 1990 amid
growing economic and social disarray. His one-party rule had become increasingly authoritarian, and hundreds of persons protest-
ing austerity measures were detained. In March 1990, hundreds of
students demanding the president's resignation clashed with police.)

Similarly, Zimbabwe still enjoys the legacy of Ian Smith's white
Rhodesia. Although Prime Minister Robert Mugabe is a professed
Marxist, he has been reluctant to dismantle the white economy he
inherited, and Zimbabwe relatively is doing well. In 1992, his rule
was threatened not by politics but by a devastating drought in
southern Africa.

FREE PRESS MODEL

During the past quarter century of one-party and/or military
rule, it was not fashionable for political leaders to advocate the free
press model of journalism for Africa. And yet, as a professional
value and legal concept, the idea of free and independent newspapers has long been valued and emulated by African journalists
themselves and by other Africans seeking just and democratic societies.

African newspapers have been directed by an impressive number of outstanding journalists, such as Hilary Ng'weno, Peter Enahoro, John Dumoga, Kelvin Mlenga, Percy Qoboza, Frene Ginwala,
Nnamdi Azikiwe, Lawrence Gandar, Dunston Kamana, to name just
a few, and these talented and courageous journalists have fought for
such values, albeit usually unsuccessfully. Even though their own
political leaders will not brook opposition or diverse views and will
support repressive press measures in UNESCO or UN meetings, the
African journalists by and large still support the values of independ-

ent journalism. Particularly in anglophone Africa, this is a part of the legacy of colonialism; journalists learned to value and to claim for themselves the "rights of Englishmen," including freedom of the press.

The short history of the African press since the end of imperial rule seems to indicate that the best and most effective papers have been found in those few enclaves where the repressive interferences of government have been resisted and where the press has some standing in the private economic sector of society.

Much of the explanation for the vitality and vigor of mass communication in India, Singapore, and Hong Kong can be explained by the fact that the media are firmly anchored in what Heilbroner calls the "economic realm," as contrasted with the "political realm."

In time, this current thinking about communication and development—this "conventional wisdom"—will undoubtedly be replaced by new fashions in theory and ideology as the conditions of the world itself change. A major regional war—another Vietnam—a serious world recession, or possibly a global depression could severely undermine the world's current faith in free trade economies as well as democratic rule. When that might happen is impossible to foresee.

10

CONCLUSION

This book has been about success and failure in the growth of news media in several African and Asian nations. Most of the failures have been in Africa. What finally can be said about the false start for Africa's press?

I believe there is no single explanation; numerous factors contributed to the failure of newspapers and other media of independent Africa to grow and prosper. Most of all, perhaps, the African media were victimized by their own governments. One-party governments and military juntas would not tolerate independent, outspoken newspapers and other voices of public opinion. The record of suppression is clear; it began soon after independence and has continued.

Further, political economies in Africa based on centralized planning and parastatal organizations left little breathing space for independent voices and media supported by the private sector. In many states, all the major instruments of public communication—daily newspapers, weeklies, television, radio, news agencies, and information services—were themselves in and of the political realm, which dominated life in the urban areas.

From 1970 onward, the deteriorating social environment of much of Africa—declining economies, political disarray, falling living standards, and general malaise—severely constrained the potential growth of media.

The picture was not uniformly bleak. In a few great cities— Lagos, Nairobi, Johannesburg, Cape Town, Dakar—the press has shown some vigor. And in those cities were newspapers—*Rand*

Daily Mail, the *Star, Daily Concord, Daily Nation, Daily Times,* and others—that had flourished for various periods under private, not government, ownership.

But, overall, media growth in Africa has been disappointing. Perhaps everyone expected too much too soon. Thirty years is just a blip in human history. Independent Africa needs more time to deal with its myriad of difficulties so that it can enter the modern world as a full partner. When it does, ideally it will be on African terms, not those of the West, whether those terms are dictated by Westminster libertarians or doctrinaire socialists.

Africa was expected to develop and modernize quickly along Western lines, and that has just not happened. Capitalism and socialism are both Western importations, and although most new nations opted for the latter, to their subsequent regret, neither approach has as yet brought real economic growth and political stablity to Africa. Perhaps an African way, one more in tune with African traditions and history, needs to be found.

Further, I believe that the persistence of traditional ways, especially the powerful forces of ethnicity, were vastly underrated by those guiding the modernization of Africa. Yet ethnicity and persistence of traditional ways are only part of the explanation for Africa's problems. Similar problems have beset India and, for other reasons, the Indians are dealing with them with somewhat more success. Nurturing the fragile flowers of mass communication in the hostile garden of Africa has proved more difficult than expected. Useful media cannot be fertilized by government ministries and political parties. The few effective newspapers and magazines have taken root in urban centers under private auspices. Africa has had too much social engineering of its media as well as of agriculture, commerce, and social relations.

But Africa is changing its ways, and the environment for independent news media may be improving if other pressing problems such as population pressures, deterioration of the environment, and economic stagnation and debt do not overwhelm the nations first. There have been encouraging signs that the leaders of Africa are making headway in putting things in order. Pragmatism is replacing ideology as African nations show more willingness to make the necessary sacrifices to revive their ailing economies.

But perhaps even more significant was the trend in 1990 and 1991 toward political changes similar to those in Eastern Europe during 1989 and 1990. After riots and demonstrations, leaders in such one-party states as Gabon, the Ivory Coast, Zaire, and Zambia all announced they would open their political systems to other parties. Prospects for democracy in these and other African nations are still quite speculative, but there was a clear thrust toward changing not just leaders but authoritarian political systems. African journalism will obviously benefit from such change.

As one who believes in the value of independent journalism, it has been dispiriting to watch despots and arbitrary leaders harass, repress, and reject efforts of African journalists to report the news and to play a role in public affairs, however imperfect those efforts may have been.

The African press in general is not a free press; in most nations, the few daily newspapers are kept and controlled instruments of unelected or unpopular governments, which can usually be changed only by a coup d'état.

A vital, free, and effective press that truly serves the needs of Africans can play an important role in aiding the rebuilding of African societies.

LESSONS FROM ASIA

The world of the 1990s certainly will be different from that of the 1960s and 1970s. With the benefit of hindsight, we can perhaps understand why the media have done well in some countries and so badly in others. Despite the high hopes of the 1950s, few nations of the Third World have lived up to their expectations.

We have looked at three Asian societies that have done well, and despite their obvious differences from anglophone Africa, India, Singapore, and Hong Kong do offer some lessons for Africa.

In over 40 years of independence, India has proved that a huge, complex nation beset with deep problems can somehow survive as the world's largest democracy. Some of the success for that survival is due to a press that was born free in 1947 (due to its inheritance from the British Raj) and because enough Indian journalists have fought doggedly over the years to maintain their freedom despite occasional official efforts to suppress newspapers and journalists. India's press is protected by its constitution and laws, something sorely lacking in much of Africa and the Third World.

Political freedom has encouraged the growth of Indian media but so has the political unity of the subcontinent, which has made possible truly national newspapers and newsmagazines and now nationwide television. This mass (and massive) market for the media has prospered in recent years, partly because of India's subtle shift from a socialist to a market-oriented economy. India is still beset with seemingly intractable problems, but its open communication system makes India better able to deal with them.

The example of Singapore would seem to send mixed signals to struggling African nations. Its spectacular economic expansion, taking its people from poverty to affluence in a generation, has been achieved behind a mere facade of democracy. The one-man rule of the brilliant Lee Kuan Yew has provided astute economic guidance but brooked no political diversity. In "Singapore, Inc.," the mass media and their audiences have prospered and proliferated as they have in the similarly successful corporate states of South Korea and Taiwan.

Have these economic miracles of Asia (Singapore, South Korea, and Taiwan) demonstrated that economic growth and media development can be achieved without free expression and democracy? Perhaps, but for how long? Economic growth and expanded mass communications also seem to arouse in people strong desires for more just and democratic societies and an increasing concern for human rights.

Hong Kong is, of course, the most special case of all and probably the most ephemeral since the offshore British colony is rapidly evolving back into being the principal metropolis of Guandong Province years before it formally returns to China in 1997.[1] Hong Kong has provided for the developing world—and Hong Kong was poor and disorganized 25 years ago—an example of how mass media can prosper and flourish when they enjoy the freedom and opportunity to do what they wish to do. Hong Kong shows that when a benign government leaves the press alone and when business opportunities to make money are freely available, some rather impressive growth and expansion can occur in mass communication. Special case? Yes, but what has happened in Hong Kong could surely happen elsewhere in the world. Hong Kong has shown what is possible.

The central conclusion of this study, then, is that the press and other media do best in free market capitalistic societies. The finest newspapers, the most stimulating broadcasting, and the best informed and interested audiences are found in those nations where the mass media are clearly located in the economic realm, as distinct from the political realm of a society. Only under capitalism, according to Robert Heilbroner, is there the clear distinction between the realm that runs the economy and the realm that governs.[2] In most African nations, as well as in socialist nations, the political realm dominates economic activity and the private business sector is too small and vulnerable to support an adequate system of mass communication. In the postwar world, the media have usually stagnated under socialist and military governments where the political and economic realms have coincided.

Also, ideally, a privately run media system should be in an open democratic society, as in India, not under authoritarian controls, as in Lee Kuan Yew's Singapore, or subject to the harsh official repressions that have been imposed on South Africa's press. A private media system without democracy and human rights can become a hollow, kept media system, as in Singapore. My opinion is that an independent media system flourishes best in an open and pluralistic society, and that is the kind of society that the people of Singapore (and other places in the world) seem to want but do not yet have. A prosperous capitalistic press has little soul when it must exist in such places as Hitler's Germany, Pinochet's Chile, or Peron's Argentina.

The world is always changing, perhaps faster today than at any time in history. Despite the myriad problems that the media daily point out to the world, there are some encouraging trends moving about the globe. Among them are growing demands from the world's peoples for better and more informative newspapers and other media of communication. And free, independent news media are essential to help us deal with our dangerous, imperiled, and interdependent world.

NOTES

CHAPTER 1

1. See Rosalynde Ainslie, *The Press in Africa: Communications Past and Present*, New York: Walker, 1966; William Hachten, *Muffled Drums: The News Media in Africa*, Ames: Iowa State University Press, 1971; Frank Barton, *The Press of Africa: Persecution and Perseverance*, New York: Africana, 1979; Dennis L. Wilcox, *Mass Media in Black Africa: Philosophy and Control*, New York: Praeger, 1975; Graham Mytton, *Mass Communication in Africa*, London: Edward Arnold, 1983; Martin Ochs, *The African Press*, Cairo: American University Press, 1986.

2. Two influential books on communication and development were Daniel Lerner, *The Passing of Traditional Society*, Glencoe: The Free Press, 1958 and Wilbur Schramm, *Mass Media and National Development*, Stanford: Stanford University Press, 1964.

3. See David Lamb, *The Africans*, New York: Random House, 1982; Martin Meredith, *The First Dance of Freedom: Black Africa in the Postwar Era*, New York: Harper and Row, 1984; Sanford Ungar, *Africa: The People and Politics of an Emerging Continent*; New York: Simon and Schuster, 1986; and Mort Rosenblum and Doug Williamson, *Squandering Eden: Africa at the Edge*, New York: Harcourt, Brace, Jovanovich, 1987. All these books are by journalists with extensive experience in Africa.

4. Helen Kitchen, *The Press in Africa*, Washington, D.C.: Ruth Sloan Associates, 1956.

5. U.S. Information Agency, *Communications Data Book for Africa*, Washington, D.C.: Government Printing Office, 1966.

6. Hachten, *Muffled Drums*, p. 24.

7. Barton, *The Press of Africa*, p. 11.

8. George Kurian, ed., *World Press Encyclopedia*, New York: Facts on File, 1981.

9. Quoted in William Hachten, *World News Prism*, 3rd ed., Ames: Iowa State University Press, 1992, p. xx.

CHAPTER 2

1. Sudan gained its independence in 1956, Ghana in 1957, and 16 other nations won political freedom in 1960. Zimbabwe did not join the others until 1980.

2. John Williams, quoted in Mytton, *Mass Communication in Africa*, p. 51.

3. James S. Coleman, *Nigeria: Background to Nationalism*, Berkeley: University of California Press, 1963, pp. 184–86. See also Fred Omu, *Press and Politics in Nigeria 1880–1937*, London: Longman, 1978.

4. William Hachten and C. Anthony Giffard, *The Press and Apartheid: Repression and Propaganda in South Africa*, Madison: University of Wisconsin Press, 1984.

5. Allister Sparks, quoted in Hachten and Giffard, *The Press and Apartheid*, p. 144.

6. Ibid. See also Les Switzer and Donna Switzer, *The Black Press in South Africa and Lesotho*, Boston: G. K. Hall, 1979.

7. Hachten, *Muffled Drums*, pp. 183–85.

8. See *Report on the Press in West Africa*, Ibadan: University College, 1960. It shows how developed and diverse the press was in West Africa during the years just before independence.

CHAPTER 3

1. Xan Smiley, "Misunderstanding Africa," *Atlantic Monthly*, September 1982, p. 70.

2. Quoted in William Hachten, "Newspapers in Africa: Change or Decay?" *Africa Report*, December 1970, p. 25.

3. Ainslie, *The Press in Africa*, p. 11.

4. William Hachten, "Ghana's Press under the N.R.C.: An Authoritarian Model for Africa," *Journalism Quarterly* 52, no. 3 (Autumn 1975): 459–60.

5. See Hachten, *Muffled Drums*, p. 154, and Barton, *The Press of Africa*, pp. 38–39.

6. Hachten, *Muffled Drums*, pp. 150ff.

7. Mytton, *Mass Communication in Africa*, pp. 92–93.

8. Hachten, "Ghana's Press," pp. 458–64.

9. Lamb, *The Africans*, pp. 244–45.

10. Ibid.

11. Hilary Ng'weno, "The Third World Dilemma: Can a State Press Be Free?" *The Weekly Review* (Nairobi), 22 June 1979.

12. Andrew Bredin, "His Master's Voice," *Index on Censorship*, May 1982, p. 3.

13. See Hachten, *World News Prism*, p. 34, and Denis McQuail, *Mass Communication Theory*, Beverly Hills: Sage, pp. 84–98.

14. Nkrumah, quoted in Ainslie, *The Press in Africa*, pp. 99–100.

15. Mytton, *Mass Communication in Africa*, p. 67.

16. Dennis L. Wilcox, "What Hope for the Press in Africa?" *Freedom at Issue*, March/April 1977, p. 12. These views were based on interviews with press attachés of African embassies in Washington, D.C.

CHAPTER 4

1. Quoted by Flora Lewis in her "Foreign Affairs" column, *New York Times*, 30 October 1988, p. 23.
2. Meredith, *The First Dance of Freedom*, p. 377.
3. Ibid.
4. "A Continent Gone Wrong," *Time*, 16 January 1984, p. 26.
5. George Ayittey, "African Freedom of Speech," *Index on Censorship*, January 1987, p. 16.
6. James Brooke, "In Africa, Tribal Hatreds Defy the Borders of State," *New York Times*, 28 August 1988, sec. 3, p. 3.
7. Kenneth Freed, "Commonwealth Ripped for Abuses," *The Capital Times*, 12 October 1987, p. 9.
8. Richard J. Barnet, "But What About Africa?" *Harper's Magazine*, May 1990, p. 45.
9. Lewis H. Gann and Peter Duignan, "Africa: Mirage or Reality," *Baltimore Sun*, 11 April 1980.
10. Lester Brown, *State of the World 1986*, New York: Norton, 1986, p. 177.
11. John C. Whitehead, "The African Economic Crisis," U.S. Department of State, Bureau of Public Affairs, Current Policy no. 757.
12. "Something Better Out of Africa," *New York Times*, 5 June 1986, p. 30.
13. Rosenblum and Williamson, *Squandering Eden*, p. 11.
14. Roberta Cohen, "Censorship Costs Lives," *Index on Censorship*, May 1987, p. 15.
15. Smiley, "Misunderstanding Africa," p. 75.
16. Ibid.
17. Ibid., p. 70.
18. Colin Legum, "Africa's journalists battle uphill to get and keep press freedoms," *Christian Science Monitor*, 24 November 1986, p. 13.
19. Iain McLellan, "TV's Shortcomings in Africa," *World Press Review*, January 1987, p. 60.
20. Ibid.

CHAPTER 5

1. Circulation figures based on estimates between March and July 1986 and supplied by Doyin Abiola, managing editor of Concord Press of Nigeria, Ltd.
2. Alan Cowell, "Free Press for Africans: Walking a Narrow Line," *New York Times*, 13 May 1983, p. 4.
3. "Nigeria," *CPJ Update*, September/October 1985, p. 7.
4. James Brooke, "Lagos Editor's Death Embarrasses Leaders, Sets Rumors Swirling," *International Herald Tribune*, 7 January 1987, p. 1.
5. For a view of media/government relations leading up to the current situation, see Hachten and Giffard, *The Press and Apartheid*.
6. See Switzer and Switzer, *The Black Press in South Africa and Lesotho*, for the history of the black press. For more recent developments, see

John Phelan, *Apartheid Media,* Westport: Lawrence Hill, 1987, and William Finnegan, *Dateline: Soweto,* New York: Harper and Row, 1988.

7. Robert Heilbroner, "The Triumph of Capitalism," *The New Yorker,* 23 January 1989, pp. 98–109.

CHAPTER 6

1. Ved Mehta, "Letter from New Delhi," *The New Yorker,* 19 September 1988, p. 114.

2. "Push Comes to Shove: A Survey of India," *The Economist,* 9–15 May 1987, p. 11.

3. Ibid.

4. K. E. Eapen, "The Indian Media Scenario" (paper presented to the International Television Studies Conference, 1986), p. 4.

5. Ibid., p. 5.

6. Mehta, "Letter," p. 114.

7. "Push Comes to Shove," p. 18.

8. Barbara Crossette, "Indian Editors Attack Defamation Bill, *New York Times,* 4 September 1988, p. 8.

9. Salamat Ali, "Persecute the Publisher," *Far Eastern Economic Review,* 26 November 1987, p. 51.

10. Roland Wolseley, ed., *Journalism in Modern India,* New York: Asia Publishing House, 1964, p. 24.

11. M. W. Desai, "Images of the Indian Press," *India News,* 28 January 1985, p. 4.

12. Eapen, "Indian Media," p. 9.

13. Ibid., 8.

14. "Indian Television Network Largest in the World?" *AMIC Bulletin* 18, no. 4 (November–December 1988): 13.

15. Ibid.

16. William K. Stevens, "India TV Boom, Reruns and Politics," *New York Times,* 27 September 1984, p. 5.

CHAPTER 7

1. This chapter is based in part on interviews and research conducted by the author in Singapore in February 1987.

2. Interview with Dr. Chan Heng Chee of National University of Singapore, February 1987.

3. In 1986, Singapore shocked the Asian business community by expelling a British merchant bank, Jardine Fleming, for giving what the government deemed bad advice.

4. Chan Heng Chee, *The Dynamics of One Party Dominance: The PAP at the Grass Roots,* Singapore: National University of Singapore, 1972, pp. 205–6. An authoritative discussion of the 1971 vendetta is contained in Anthony Polsky, "Lee Kuan Yew versus the Press," *Pacific Community,* October 1971, pp. 183–203.

5. Colin Campbell, "Singapore Pulls in Reins on the Press," *New York Times,* 20 July 1982, p. 4.

6. Eddie C. Y. Kuo, "Communication Policies and National Development," in P. Chen, ed., *Singapore: Development Policies and Trends,* Kuala Lumpur: Oxford University Press, 1983, p. 268.

7. Monthly circulation report of Straits Times Press, January 1987.

8. "Singapore's Chinese Press Enjoys Boom," *AMIC Bulletin,* March–April 1988, p. 12.

9. Nigel Holloway, "A Fall from Grace," *Far Eastern Economic Review,* January 22 1987, p. 31.

10. Kuo, "Communication Policies," p. 269.

11. Interview with Lim Heng, public relations head of SBC, in February 1987.

12. To quote a Lee partisan: "While the Communists took on the PAP in the field organizations, party branches, etc.—through mass rallies, loudspeaker vans, and pamphlets—the ruling party (PAP) fought back with a new weapon, television. Communists, pro-communists and their front organizations were exposed, their agitation, their intimidating tactics—strikes, demonstrations, and riots—were revealed to the people through television. . . . On the fateful day of 21 July 1964, Singapore had its first racial riots. Curfews were imposed and there were no newspapers, no talks in coffee shops and no pavement strolls. The island was paralyzed. Television and radio (controlled by Lee) provided the only link between the government and the people, and kept the people informed and their morale high." (From Dr. Ow Chin Hock, "Broadcasting in Singapore," *People's Action Party,* Anniversary Issue, 1979, p. 136.)

13. Lee has made extensive use of the media in various public information campaigns, such as those to "Speak Mandarin," avoid littering, encourage family planning, and, more recently, encourage the better educated to have more children. Although Lee has long been an implacable foe of Communist China, his campaigns have borne a striking resemblance to those of Maoist China.

14. Survey Research Group, "Singapore Leads VCR Ownership," *AMIC Bulletin,* March/April 1988, p. 12.

15. Kuo, "Communication Policies," p. 271.

16. See Barbara Crossette, "Singapore Opposition Finding the Mood Tougher," *New York Times,* 12 May 1988, p. 1.

17. Interview with Steven Duthie, *Asian Wall Street Journal,* in Singapore, February 1987.

18. Margaret Scott, "A Meeting of Minds," *Far Eastern Economic Review,* 27 October 1988, p. 18.

19. Several foreign correspondents interviewed by this author said they considered that Singapore had become a much less free place to report news than either Malaysia or Indonesia and well behind the Philippines and Thailand, the most open for foreign journalists. Despite Singapore's excellent airline connections and agreeable living conditions, Bangkok is becoming a more popular venue for resident correspondents in Southeast Asia.

20. V. G. Kulkarni, "A Big Push for Publishing," *Far Eastern Economic Review,* 3 July 1986, p. 28.

21. This source requested anonymity.

22. See Lerner, *The Passing of Traditional Society,* pp. 64, 85. Aside from this difference, Singapore seems to be an affirmation of the dominant

paradigm of communication development espoused by Daniel Lerner, Wilbur Schramm, and other communication scholars during the 1960s and so widely criticized during the 1970s.

23. In April 1988, speaking to the American Society of Newspaper Editors in Washington, D.C., Lee said the American concept of freedom of the press could bring turmoil to Singapore. "I am Asia. I am not America. I cannot allow American correspondents to decide my national agenda for me," he said. (Quoted by Anthony Lewis in *New York Times*, 22 May 1988, 29.)

CHAPTER 8

1. Peter Bauer, *Equality, The Third World and Economic Delusion*, Cambridge: Harvard University Press, 1981, p. 186.

2. Ibid.

3. Interview with Raymond Wong, news controller of TVB, April 1987. Wong has worked at a U.S. television station.

4. Interview with T. W. Leung of Commercial Radio, 15 April 1987.

5. Interview in April 1987 with two U.S. diplomats who requested anonymity.

6. Louise do Rosario, "The Heavies Struggle to Make Ends Meet," *Far Eastern Economic Review*, 13 February 1988, p. 30.

7. Jim Jubak, "Paper Tiger," *Northwest Portfolio*, July 1988, p. 23.

8. Emily Lau, "The News Media," in *Hong Kong in Transition*, ed. Joseph Cheng, Hong Kong: Oxford University Press, 1986, pp. 420–21.

9. Ibid.

10. Emily Lau, "A Media Melting Pot of All Political Stripes," *Far Eastern Economic Review*, 13 February 1986, pp. 26–29.

11. Interview with Miranda Yiu in Hong Kong, April 1987.

12. Lau, "The News Media," p. 446.

13. Laurence Zuckerman, " 'False News' Law is No Balm to Jittery Hong Kong," *CPJ Update*, May/June 1987, p. 4.

14. Frank Ching, "Hong Kong Plays Political Censor for China," *Asian Wall Street Journal*, 17 March 1987, p. 1.

15. Interview with Fred Zimmerman, editor and publisher of the *Asian Wall Street Journal*, 22 April 1987, in Hong Kong.

16. Interview with Patrick Smith in Hong Kong, April 1987.

17. Zimmerman, interview.

18. Julia Leung, "China Gets a Better Press in Hong Kong," *Asian Wall Street Journal*, 7 January 1986, p. 1.

19. Interview with Derek Davies in Hong Kong, 14 April 1987.

20. Sheryl WuDunn, "By Hong Kong Measure, 1997 Is Any Day Now," *New York Times*, 15 March 1992, Sec. E, p. 4.

CHAPTER 9

1. Lester Thurow, *Dangerous Currents: The State of Economics*, New York: Random House, 1983, introduction.

2. Bauer, *Equality, The Third World and Economic Delusion*, p. 1.

3. Ithiel Pool, "What Ferment? A Challenge for Empirical Research," *Journal of Communication,* Summer 1983, p. 258.

4. Heilbroner, "The Triumph of Capitalism," p. 98.

5. Smiley, "Misunderstanding Africa," pp. 73–74.

6. Ibid.

7. Clifford D. May, "Africa's Men in Khaki Are Often a Law unto Themselves," *New York Times,* 6 October 1985, p. 69.

8. Hachten, "Ghana's Press," pp. 458–64.

9. See Hachten, *World News Prism,* and McQuail, *Mass Communication Theory,* for discussion of the developmental concept of the press.

10. The classic work is Daniel Lerner's *The Passing of Traditional Society.* Many other related studies followed. See bibliography of Fred Frey's article, "Communication and Development," in *Handbook of Communication,* ed. Wilbur Schramm and Ithiel Pool, Chicago: Rand McNally, 1973, for a list of the major studies.

11. See Mustapha Masmoudi, "The New World Information Order," a paper for the International Commission for the Study of Communication Problems, Paris: UNESCO, 1978.

12. James Brooke, "Ivory Coast: African Success Story Built on Rich Farms and Stable Politics," *New York Times,* 26 April 1988, p. 8.

CHAPTER 10

1. Nicholas Kristof, "Hong Kong and China Grow Close," *New York Times,* 12 February 1989, p. 3.

2. Heilbroner, "The Triumph of Capitalism," pp. 98–109.

SELECTED BIBLIOGRAPHY

Ainslie, Rosalynde. *The Press in Africa: Communications Past and Present.* New York: Walker, 1966.

Ayittey, George. "African Freedom of Speech." *Index on Censorship,* January 1987, p. 16.

Barton, Frank. *The Press of Africa: Persecution and Perseverance.* New York: Africana, 1979.

Bredin, Andrew. "His Master's Voice." *Index on Censorship,* May 1982, p. 3.

Brooke, James. "Lagos Editor's Death Embarrasses Leaders, Sets Rumors Swirling." *International Herald Tribune,* 7 January 1987, p. 1.

Brown, Lester. *State of the World 1986.* New York: W. W. Norton, 1986.

Cohen, Roberta. "Censorship Costs Lives." *Index on Censorship,* May 1987, p. 15.

Coleman, James S. *Nigeria: Background to Nationalism.* Berkeley: University of California Press, 1963.

Cowell, Alan. "Free Press for Africans: Walking a Narrow Line." *New York Times,* 13 May 1983, p. 4.

Eapen, K. E. "The India Media Scenario." Paper presented at the International Television Studies Conference, 1986.

Faringer, Gunilla L. *Press Freedom in Africa.* New York: Praeger, 1991.

Finnegan, William. *Dateline: Soweto.* New York: Harper and Row, 1988.

Frey, Fred. "Communication and Development." In *Handbook of Communication,* ed. Wilbur Schramm and Ithiel Pool. Chicago: Rand McNally, 1973, pp. 337–461.

Hachten, William. *Muffled Drums: The News Media in Africa.* Ames: Iowa State University Press, 1971.

_____. *World News Prism: Changing Media of International Communication,* 3rd ed. Ames: Iowa State University Press, 1992.

_____ and C. Anthony Giffard. *The Press and Apartheid: Repression and Propaganda in South Africa.* Madison: University of Wisconsin Press, 1984.

Hawk, Beverly G. (ed.) *Africa's Media Image.* New York: Praeger, 1992.

Heilbroner, Robert. "The Triumph of Capitalism." *The New Yorker,* 23 January 1989, pp. 98–109.

Kitchen, Helen. *The Press in Africa.* Washington, D.C.: Ruth Sloan Associates, 1956.

Kurian, George, ed. *World Press Encyclopedia.* New York: Facts on File, 1981.

Lamb, David. *The Africans.* New York: Random House, 1982.

Lau, Emily. "The News Media." In *Hong Kong in Transition*, ed. Joseph Cheng. Hong Kong: Oxford University Press, 1986.

Lerner, Daniel. *The Passing of Traditional Society*. Glencoe: The Free Press, 1958.

McLellan, Iain. "TV's Shortcomings in Africa." *World Press Review*, January 1987, p. 60.

McQuail, Denis. *Mass Communication Theory*. Beverly Hills: Sage, 1983.

Mehta, Ved. "Letter from New Delhi." *The New Yorker*, 19 September 1988, p. 114.

Meredith, Martin. *The First Dance of Freedom: Black Africa in the Postwar Era*. New York: Harper and Row, 1984.

Mytton, Graham. *Mass Communication in Africa*. London: Arnold, 1983.

Ochs, Martin. *The African Press*. Cairo: American University Press, 1986.

Phelan, John. *Apartheid Media*. Westport: Lawrence Hill, 1987.

Polsky, Anthony. "Lee Kuan Yew versus the Press." *Pacific Community*, October 1971, pp. 183–203.

"Push Comes to Shove: A Survey of India." *The Economist*, 9–15 May 1987.

Rosenblum, Mort, and Doug Williamson. *Squandering Eden: Africa at the Edge*. New York: Harcourt, Brace, Jovanovich, 1987.

Schramm, Wilbur. *Mass Media and National Development*. Stanford: Stanford University Press, 1964.

Smiley, Xan. "Misunderstanding Africa." *Atlantic Monthly*, September 1982, pp. 70–79.

Stevenson, Robert L. *Communication, Development and the Third World*. New York: Longman, 1988.

Ungar, Sanford. *Africa: The People and Politics of an Emerging Continent*. New York: Simon and Schuster, 1986.

Wilcox, Dennis. *Mass Media in Black Africa: Philosophy and Control*. New York: Praeger, 1975.

INDEX